MUNGO'S TONGUES

Ann Street, 1965 (John S. Logan) MITCHELL LIBRARY

MUNGO'S TONGUES

GLASGOW POEMS
1630 — 1990

Edited by

HAMISH WHYTE

MAINSTREAM
PUBLISHING

EDINBURGH AND LONDON

For Helen and Alan Durndell

First published in Great Britain in 1993 by
MAINSTREAM PUBLISHING COMPANY (EDINBURGH) LTD
7 Albany Street
Edinburgh EH1 3UG

ISBN 1 85158 580 X

A catalogue record for this book is available from the British Library

The publisher gratefully acknowledges the financial assistance of
The Scottish Arts Council in the production of this volume.

Typeset in Ehrhardt by Servis Filmsetting Ltd, Manchester

Printed in Great Britain by The Cromwell Press, Melksham, Wiltshire

Contents

Acknowledgments

I am grateful to all the authors, past and present, whose work is in this book (and whose work is not); and to the copyright holders who so generously gave permission for poems to be included. For suggestions, pointers, help in tracing poems, poets and illustrations, specific assistance and general encouragement, many thanks to Moira Burgess, Jim Clayson, Robert Crawford, Anne Escott, Ian Gordon, Iain and Jean Hamilton, Philip Hobsbaum, Hugues Journès, H. Gustav Klaus, Tom Leonard, Maurice Lindsay, Brian McCabe, Bernadette McCann, Robert McCahill, Margery McCulloch, Janette McGinn, Adam McNaughtan, Hazel Miller, Edwin Morgan (not least for the title), Cordelia Oliver, Dilys Rose, Enda Ryan, Brian Skillen (still searching for the Three Partick Mice), Gael Turnbull, Leslie J. Verth, my mother Alicia Whyte, and my colleagues in the Mitchell Library's Rare Books and Manuscripts Department: Hazel Wright, Anne McPherson and Linda Burke.

I am especially grateful to Simon Berry, Joe Fisher and Kevin McCarra for reading the text, for their useful comments and for letting their encyclopaedic brains be picked.

Acknowledgments must go to Glasgow City Libraries, in particular the Glasgow Collection and the Language and Literature Department of the Mitchell Library. Without their collection of local literature, built up by librarians over the 116 years of the Mitchell's existence, my task would have been so much harder: a wonderful resource.

Thanks too to the nice Mainstream people: Bill, Claire, Judy, Janene and Neil. And thanks, as ever, to Winifred, for seeing me through the press.

For permission to reprint copyright material the editor and publisher gratefully acknowledge the following: Tom Berry for 'Gorbals'; Ron Butlin for 'The City Cemetery'; Stewart Conn for 'Family Visit', 'Ghosts' and extract from 'A Sense of Order', reproduced by permission of Bloodaxe Books Ltd from *In the Kibble Palace* by Stewart Conn (Bloodaxe Books, 1987); Cath Craig for 'Glasgow's Alive'; Robert Crawford for 'Parachuting into Glasgow' and Robert Crawford and Chatto & Windus for 'Inner Glasgow' (from *A Scottish Assembly*); Ian Hamilton Finlay for 'Glasgow Beasts, an a Burd'; Jean Hamilton for 'News of the World' by Iain Hamilton; Nora Hunter for 'Lament for a Lost Dinner Ticket' by Margaret Hamilton; Robin Hamilton for 'The Girl I Met in Byres Road'; Alan Jackson for 'glasgow's full of artists'; William Keys for 'A Dug A Dug'; David Kinloch for 'Joan Eardley'; Hilary Kirk and David H. Kirk for 'Ode to the Clyde' by Charles J. Kirk; Frank Kuppner for 'Kelvinbridge: A Node'; Tom Leonard for 'Six Glasgow Poems', 'Tea Time' and 'You have returned to Glasgow . . .'; Maurice Lindsay for 'Seen Out'; Douglas Lipton for extract from 'The Miracle of Glasgow's Cultural Revival'; Liz Lochhead and Polygon for 'The Bargain', 'Carnival', 'Obituary', 'Something I'm Not' and 'Sometimes it's Hard to be a Woman'; Michael Grieve and Carcanet Press Ltd for 'Glasgow, 1960' and 'In Glasgow' by Hugh MacDiarmid (from Hugh MacDiarmid, *Selected Poems*, eds. Michael Grieve and Alan Riach, 1992); Carl MacDougall for 'Cod Liver Oil and Orange Juice'; Janette McGinn for 'The Butchers of Glasgow' by Matt McGinn; James McGonigal for 'Plain Speaking'; Tom McGrath for 'there was that time charlie tully'; Adam McNaughtan for 'The Jeely Piece Song'; Ruaraidh MacThómais (Derick Thomson) for 'An Glaschu' and 'Sràid ann an Glaschu'; John Maley for 'The Thatcher Years'; Gerald Mangan for 'Glasgow 1956' and 'Gunfight at the Govan Corral', reproduced by permission of Bloodaxe Books Ltd from: *Waiting for the Storm* by Gerald Mangan (Bloodaxe Books, 1990); William Montgomerie for 'Glasgow Street'; Edwin Morgan and Carcanet Press Ltd for 'By the Preaching of the Word', 'Glasgow Green', 'Glasgow Sonnets', 'In Glasgow', 'King Billy', 'On John Maclean' and 'Rider' (from Edwin Morgan, *Collected Poems*, 1990) and Edwin Morgan and Mariscat Press for 'A City', 'Clydegrad' and 'Matt McGinn'; Mrs Ethel E. Ross and Mrs Irene H. Abenheimer for 'Industrial Scene' by Edwin Muir; Stephen Mulrine for 'The Coming of the Wee Malkies', 'Nostalgie' and 'A Glasgow Cassandra'; Michael Munro for 'Carbolic Dan'; Ranald MacColl and the Neill family for 'Perishin' Poem' by Bud Neill; David Neilson for 'To Lesbia's Husband'; Donny O'Rourke for 'Great Western Road'; Tom Scott for 'James Maxton'; Iain Crichton Smith and Carcanet Press Ltd for 'Glasgow' and 'You Lived in Glasgow' (from *Collected Poems*, 1992); the Trustees of the National Library of Scotland for 'Symbol' by William Soutar; Alan Spence for 'Jingle'; Anne Stevenson for 'Pigeons in George Square'; Valerie Thornton for 'Birds of Passage'; John Carswell for 'Glasgow, Easter 1968' by Joan Ure; Kenneth White and Mainstream Publishing for 'Glasgow'; Brian Whittingham for 'Journeyman'.

I have been unable to trace copyright holders for the poems by Edward Hunter, W. J. F. Hutcheson, John Kincaid, Jean Milton and Iain Nicolson. Any information, corrections, etc. will be gratefully received to set the record straight in future editions.

Thanks are due to Mrs James Black for permission to reproduce the Joan Eardley picture, to Ian Fleming for permission to reproduce his etching of the Botanic Gardens and to Alasdair Gray for the cover painting. The photographing of these pictures was done by the late George Oliver; a selection of his Glasgow photographs is included as a tribute to him and his work – just a tiny fraction of the record George quietly built up of the city and its people through the changes of the last 30 years. I am immensely grateful to Cordelia Oliver, not only for permission to reproduce George's photographs, but also for the generosity of spirit in which she gave permission and for the time and trouble she went to in this and other matters (not to mention her hospitality); thanks too to Flora Ritchie for printing.

Thanks also to Valerie Thornton, Edwin Morgan and Robert Walker for their photographs.

All other illustrations are taken from the collections of the Mitchell Library, Glasgow. I am grateful to Glasgow City Libraries for permission to reproduce these and for providing copies, in particular to the former Assistant Director (Reference Services) Jim Mahon and his successor Fionna MacPherson. Special thanks to Moira Thorburn of the Graphics Department for photography. And thanks also in this respect to Robert McFarlane of Glasgow City Libraries Publications Board (co-publishers of *Noise and Smoky Breath*).

Introduction

Gaudet glasgu praecipue:
tanto pollens sub presule:
tellus iam plaudit scotica:
sancti cernens insignia

(Office of S. Kentigern from Breviarum Aberdonense
printed by Walter Chepman, Edinburgh, 1509)

Mungo, the patron saint of Glasgow, who settled there in the sixth century, may have composed poems – he is certainly supposed to have chanted psalms while immersed in the Molendinar burn – but nothing by him has survived. There is the story of Columba visiting Kentigern (Mungo's real name) and composing a hymn while there and exchanging holy staves with him – they may even have exchanged verses, as Edwin Morgan conjectured in his macaronic 'Colloquy in Glaschu':

God but *le son du cor*, Columba sighed
to Kentigern, *est triste au fond silvarum!*
Frater, said Kentigern, I see no harm.

Glasgow figures in the *Wallace*, a heroic poem on Scotland's national hero, written around 1477 by a minstrel known as Blind Harry (*c*.1450–92), particularly as the scene of a battle between the Scots and English at the Bell o' the Brae, on the High Street, in 1300. In the old ballad, 'Waly, Waly', Glasgow is just a town to be seen in:

When we came in by Glasgow town,
We were a comely sight to see.

It was not until the end of the seventeenth century and beginning of the eighteenth century that Glasgow became a place to write about. The first full-length book on Glasgow was John McUre's *A View of the City of Glasgow* (Glasgow, 1736), in which the city is described as standing 'deliciously' on the banks of the Clyde and 'is generally believed to be of its Bigness the most beautiful City of the World'. Glasgow was no longer a sleepy medieval ecclesiastical settlement and university town, it was now a bustling trading and manufacturing centre. Here is the beginning of that modern confidence in Glasgow shown by its citizens which reached its peak in the nineteenth century when it was the Second City of the Empire. And the city's literary history begins about this time as well, in the strains of Augustan topographical verse.

The Glasgow poet Edwin Morgan maintains that poetry should 'acknowledge its environment'. Over the last three hundred years there has been no shortage of Glasgow poets doing just that, responding in verse (good, bad and indifferent) to their personal situation, to the changing face and conditions of the city, campaigning at times for change themselves: from the elegant eighteenth-century merchant town, through the violent effects of the Industrial Revolution, to the social optimism (and despair) of the present era.

From a wide range of sources – books, pamphlets, magazines, song-sheets, chapbooks, newspapers – the inhabitants of Glasgow, and some outsiders – weavers, shoemakers, housewives, teachers, students, booksellers, pedlars, paupers, journalists, engineers, pawnbrokers, woodturners, anon. too, and even professional poets – give voice to the lives and times of a city: a testimony to its variety and energy.

In *The Glasgow Poets* (1903), George Eyre-Todd identified three previous collections of poetry in Glasgow and their contributors. The first was the series of penny numbers, *Poetry, Original and Selected*, published by the booksellers James Brash and William Reid between 1795 and 1798. Their shop in the Trongate was, Eyre-Todd says, the earliest of the many literary howffs in the city. The pamphlet's contents included poems by Burns (who knew Reid) and a version of John Mayne's 'Glasgow'. The next is the famous collection of humorous, sentimental and satirical verse, *Whistle-Binkie; or, the Piper of the Party: being a Collection of Songs for the Social Circle*, five series of which were published between 1832 and 1843, edited by John Donald Carrick and Alexander Rodger. The backshop of the publisher David Robertson in Glassford Street provided yet another howff; contributors included William Miller and William Motherwell. Then there was the Glasgow Ballad Club, founded in 1876 and only recently disbanded, which produced five volumes of less than remarkable verse between 1885 and 1952.

Another nineteenth-century group worth mentioning was that coterie loosely formed around James Hedderwick, the editor of the *Glasgow Citizen*, in the 1850s, and which included James Macfarlan, Alexander Smith, David Gray,

James P. Crawford (author of 'The Drunkard's Raggit Wean'), the miner poet David Wingate, and Hugh Macdonald; many of them feeling – as industry tightened its grip on the city, the population grew, living room shrank and the skies darkened – the stark contrast between town and country. Macfarlan was forever trying to escape the city to the country of his childhood, but its 'jarring life' was part of him and his poetry ('The city where wide-throated chimneys pour/Their black foul breath upon the blue of heaven'); Macdonald admired industrial progress, but went for rambles *round* Glasgow and penned rural lyrics.

This century there have been at least two groups of poets who took notice of their environment. First, the Clyde Group of the 1940s whose aims were political, inspired by John MacLean and a commitment to Scottish Republicanism – one of whom, Freddy Anderson, is still fighting, still writing (see his *At Glasgow Cross*, 1987). And second, that grouping of Glasgow poets which emerged in the 1960s and 1970s, not a school, but individual poets with Glasgow connections which, with a distinctly non-parochial outlook, are revealed in their work: Edwin Morgan, Tom Leonard, Liz Lochhead, Stephen Mulrine, Alan Spence, Tom McGrath and others. With hindsight it can be seen that the time was ripe for a flowering of Glasgow writing. The city was going through physical change under the Comprehensive Development Plan, 'a dramatic swerve into the modern age' (Edwin Morgan). There were varying reactions: some, like Morgan, welcomed the marching multistorey flats and looping flyovers; others expressed themselves more traditionally and nostalgically, summed up in Adam McNaughtan's 'Where is the Glasgow?' (c.f. Robert Galloway two hundred years before in his 'Glasgow Reviewed' – some things don't change). Added to the stimulus of physical renewal, the literary climate was favourable. Glasgow University was stuffed with poets (Scott, Morgan, White, Mulrine, Leonard, Spence, Macneacail *et al*); Philip Hobsbaum's flat offered a meeting place for writers to get together, read and discuss their work; Tom McGrath was organising jazz and poetry events, public readings in Exchange Square and a publishing programme with his wife Maureen.

It is perhaps easy to take this creative ferment, this tenement industry, too seriously; to look back on it as some kind of golden age of Glasgow poetry. In a way it was, but it is salutary to read the satirical account of the 1960s' poetry scene by Tom Leonard himself: 'It was the place, and the *placeness* of the place ... Every dunny was the Frontier of Art and smokeless zones let the city's poets gaze up at the stars ... And sometimes half-crazed with the very thingness of the whole thing, we'd gather in some mean old backyard at dusk, and cook trout and beans under a Glasgow moon.' (*Chapman* 43/44, 1986)

The canal connecting the rivers Forth and Clyde was begun in 1768 and completed in 1790, a tremendous work, thirty-five miles long. One of its incidental wonders was the aqueduct carrying the canal over the River Kelvin at Maryhill, the largest of its kind at that time. Someone (possibly the poet William Reid, 1764–1831, of the publishers Brash and Reid) was so impressed by this feat of engineering that he felt it had to be recorded – not in prose but in verse – hence, 'Verses on Viewing the Aqueduct Bridge', 1796. This kind of memorable speech was considered the right vehicle for describing a mechanical process such as the canal lock system. Poetry celebrated natural wonders, so why not man-made ones. Similar verse was being written in other industrial centres, for example James Bissett's 'Ramble of the Gods through Birmingham' (1800), a poetical tour of the industries of 'The Toy-Shop of the World'. Forty years later Alexander Rodger commemorated the opening of the Glasgow and Greenock Railway:

> Thy cylinder, piston and ponderous beam,
> Are the creatures of thine own creation – O Steam!

Street life in Glasgow is probably not as lively as it once was, mostly buskers and bible-thumpers now. I remember so-called 'characters' from the 1960s like 'Hitchy Feet', my grandfather saw and heard The Clincher, but the early part of last century seems to have positively teemed with eccentric beggars, musicians, poets and story-tellers, many of them patronisingly immortalised in the various reminiscences of Glasgow worthies.

Very little survives of the poetry and songs of the popular Glasgow fiddler Blind Alick Macdonald (1771–1830) beyond different (posthumous) versions of the same stray verses. He was much in demand for penny reels and weddings but was best loved for his humorous verses on the news of the day which he improvised as he walked the streets. His first effort on coming to Glasgow, about 1790, was reputedly:

> I've travell'd all the world over,
>   And many a place beside;
> But I never saw a more beautiful City,
>   Than that on the navigable river the Clyde.

His verses on the commanding officers of the Glasgow Volunteers were inspired by the grand review by the Earl of Moira of all the local volunteer forces on the Green in 1804.

Like the fiery god of war,
 Colonel Geddes does advance,
On a black horse that belong'd
 To the murder'd king of France!

Major Hunter cometh next;
 In a kilt, see he goes;
Every inch he's a man,
 From the head to the toes!

John Geddes owned the Verreville Glass Works, near the Broomielaw, and Samuel Hunter (1769–1839) was the six-foot, eighteen-stone editor of the *Glasgow Herald* (from 1803–37). The latter had another verse added later:

He is the loyal Editor,
 Of the Herald news-pa-per –
And no man at the punch bowl,
 The punch can better stir.

This series with additions ran and ran until at least 1820 and the Volunteers' glorious victory over the bloody revolutionaries of the Radical Rising. A composite piece, 'Glasgow Patriots', was printed in the first series of *Whistle-Binkie* (1832) and some of the Volunteers verses appeared in the second series (1839) in a section called 'Street Oratory' which purported to enact the kind of scene where people would gather round Blind Alick, Jamie Blue and 'Hawkie' (William Cameron) to hear them recite and to offer them challenges for extemporisation. For more on Blind Alick and others, see John Strang, *Glasgow and its Clubs* (London and Glasgow: Richard Griffin, 1856) and Peter Mackenzie, *Old Reminiscences of Glasgow and the West of Scotland*, vol. III (Glasgow: John Tweed, 1868).

Baudelaire pinpointed the essence of the attraction of the city for the poet in the middle of the nineteenth century – the artist amid the teeming millions: 'multitude and solitude: terms that an active and fertile poet can make equal and interchangeable'. The city was a 'space of vitality'; it taught the soul to 'give itself utterly, with all its poetry and charity, to the unexpectedly emergent, to the passing unknown'. As Raymond Williams describes in *The Country and the City*, this was to become a major response into the twentieth century: 'This social character of the city – its transitoriness, its unexpectedness, its essential and exciting isolation and procession of men and events – was seen as the reality of all human life . . . City experience was now becoming so widespread . . . there seemed little reality in any other mode of life; all sources of perception seemed to begin and end in the city.'

Some of Baudelaire's Scottish contemporaries seem to have been imbued with this urban poetic sensibility. Alexander Smith, in a tribute to his fellow Glasgow poet Hugh Macdonald, wrote:

> And then, to complete a poetic education, there was Glasgow herself – black river flowing between two glooms of masts – the Trongate's all-day roar of traffic, and at night the faces of the hurrying crowds brought out keenly for a moment in the light of the shop windows – the miles of stony streets, with statues in the squares and open spaces – the grand Cathedral, filled once with Popish shrines and rolling incense, on one side of the ravine, and, on the other, John Knox on his pillar, impeaching it with outstretched arm that clasps a Bible. And ever, as the darkness came, the district north-east and south of the city was filled with shifting glare and gloom of furnace fires; instead of night and its privacy, the splendour of towering flame brought to the inhabitants of the eastern and southern streets a fluctuating scarlet day, piercing nook and cranny as searchingly as any sunlight – making a candle needless to the housewife as she darned stockings for the children, and turning to a perfect waste of charm, the blush on a sweet-heart's cheek.
>
> (*A Summer in Skye*, 1865)

This is, in effect, a prose version of his poem 'Glasgow' (1854–57), a richly evocative piece on the splendour and squalor of the city. A hundred years on, it still finds echoes in the early work of Edwin Morgan:

> Black lay the bridge
> Above its drowned lamp-images; it shakes:
> A late train blazes and shrieks past. I watch
> As its train of sparks rides off into the darkness
>
> ('Northern Nocturnal', 1954)

One writer who deeply felt the alienation of cities was the strange, self-destructive Glasgow poet James Macfarlan, who died in poverty in 1862 aged thirty:

I stood at noontide 'mid the flood-like throng,
Pouring incessant through the city street

('Written in the City')

Another contemporary, the poorhouse poet John Young, perhaps gets closer to the actual bustle, activity and energy of Glasgow street life which, in his poem 'My New Location' (1864), he fills with 'masons, plumbers, joiners, sawers, moulders, potters, bottle-blawers'.

In the 1930s and 1940s Hugh MacDiarmid wrote extensively on Glasgow, usually attacking the place for apathy and mediocrity: 'Everything is dead except stupidity here'. He did not agree with Coriolanus that 'the people are the city': 'The houses are Glasgow, not the people'. Despite having lived in the city at various times, as Philip Hobsbaum has written, his invective is external: 'Great poet though he is elsewhere, he cannot get anywhere near the people ... It is as though MacDiarmid's loathing for Glasgow pre-empted any chance of his hearing the way its inhabitants talk.' (*Glasgow Magazine* 3, 1983) In a lighter moment in 1935 MacDiarmid imagined a Glasgow of the future, a centre of culture. Edwin Morgan, William Gilfedder and Tom Leonard offer some ripostes to MacDiarmid in 'Glasgow Sonnets', 'Glasgow' and 'You have returned to Glasgow . . .'. In a poem of 1936, 'Personalities and the Machine Age', MacDiarmid did find something positive in Glasgow, 'In crank-heads flashing rhythmically between / Twin columns hiding flying crossroads and thrusting silver rods', and interestingly went on to praise contemporary photographers of urban scenes as more in touch than painters with modern life.

The first edition of this anthology was criticised by some reviewers for the negative 'image' of Glasgow they thought it portrayed. But poets write what they must; for them, as for the media, decadence, dereliction and delinquency make good copy. Edwin Morgan's view is that there is 'something about violence that lends itself to drama, and poetry likes a bit of drama . . . Not that there are no other violent places than Glasgow, but it often has associations of that kind . . . You're aware also – perhaps morally dangerously or wrongly – of the aesthetic possibilities that can be drawn from violence.' (*Akros*, December 1976) Morgan's 'Glasgow Green' is as real and a part of Glasgow as Pollok Park's Burrell Collection. In *Vision of Scotland* (1948) the Glasgow-born poet G. S. Fraser wrote:

I think it says something for the vigour of the Scottish stock that the slums of Glasgow should produce even toughs and comedians, and not merely creatures without hope. I would rather see, in any human being, a dangerous or a destructive sort of vitality, than a quiet no life at all; while there is life, there is hope, and I feel there is hope for Glasgow. Dr Walter Elliot has very aptly called Glasgow 'the furious city'; in the great shipyards and foundries, that fury – which, indeed, has spread a thick black and smoky belt across the whole waist of Scotland! – has been constructive; I believe that we shall see a time when, in social life, too, its expression will be constructive energy. But at least Glasgow is not a dead city; fury, frustration, laughter, violence, these are the qualities of a living and savable soul.

And a recent poem, 'Glaswegian', by David Betteridge, ends:

She often breaks,
but from the fracture in her soul
there leaps a scorching flame of life.

What, it is sometimes asked, is so special or different about Glasgow poetry (or fiction or whatever)? Could it not be set anywhere and still have the same impact, does it have to be labelled 'Glasgow'? There is something in this, but writers often address a specific local issue which may well have a wider application. Because something is local it need not be parochial. 'All creative art,' wrote D. H. Lawrence, 'must rise out of specific soil and flicker with a spirit of place.' There are several poems in this anthology entitled 'In Glasgow'. Do they need to be in anywhere?

Consider the one by Edwin Morgan, a love poem, almost song. The title must be significant, otherwise it might be 'In a Room' or something of that sort. A clue is the reference to Easterhouse, the Glasgow housing scheme synonymous with deprivation. To those who protest that knowledge of Easterhouse must only be local, 'Glasgow' in the title should be enough to signal something of the nature of Easterhouse, given Glasgow's usual reputation. That the person in the poem should be described as 'shy' is traditional, but Morgan's reference to Easterhouse seems to revitalise that old conceit, if in a rather chilling manner. The mention of chains and Easterhouse (which recalls Edwin Muir's 1930s definition of a Glasgow slum as 'a sort of invisible cage, whose bars are as strong as iron') can only make us wonder whether the uneasiness of the person described is more than temporary. Society, then, intrudes into a poem which would otherwise have been simply a lightweight celebration. This kind of thing is at work in the poems of Robin Hamilton and Liz Lochhead, among others.

The anthology is not intended as a poetical history of Glasgow. From a local studies point of view the poems can be adduced as evidence along with other human documents, such as burgh records, official reports, maps, photographs, statistics, census returns, sasines, estate and business records, directories, histories, newspapers, diaries, parish registers and all the rest. The poems are more of a kind of character witness, offering personal, partial, biased views of people or events, perhaps, but authentic nonetheless.

I have chosen poems I felt had something interesting, surprising, humorous to say, of relevance to Glasgow and Glaswegians; poems I thought deserved to be rescued, poems worth at least one more reading since their burial in some short-lived magazine; and poems that simply appealed to me for one reason or another.

Mungo's Tongues is a revised and expanded edition of the 1983 collection *Noise and Smoky Breath*, which was devoted to twentieth-century poetry only. The present anthology not only includes the highlights of the earlier book, but gathers together some neglected or forgotten material and also brings the poetic survey of Glasgow up to date.

There are various themes or threads, some more apparent than others, such as the emphasis on people. One theme consciously pursued was the poetical use made of the Glasgow coat of arms and its accompanying rhyme and motto: there have been several variations over the last few hundred years, from Robert Main's '*salmo maris, terraeque arbos, avis aeris*' of *c*.1630 (not included), to Andrew Park's 'Let Glasgow Flourish!' (1842) and the more recent 'By the Preaching of the Word' by Edwin Morgan (1974) and Alan Spence's 'Jingle' (1981).

I have had to leave out many poems I would have liked to include, for various reasons, mainly lack of space. There will be poems omitted which readers may have confidently expected to find. They will have their own favourites and are free to compile their own anthology. If I were to redo the collection it might well be radically different. I would here echo Roger Lonsdale in his introduction to his brilliant anthology *The New Oxford Book of Eighteenth-Century Verse* (paperback 1987), who felt haunted by the memory of the men and women whose literary bones he had disturbed after two hundred years for whom he had 'envisaged some kind of minor literary resurrection, but who necessarily fell back into the darkness of the centuries'. He added 'perhaps irretrievably', but I would hope this anthology might encourage further discovery, archaeology not in tombs but in tomes.

The poems are arranged chronologically: either according to the date of composition, where known, or date of first publication or first significant appearance. One disadvantage of this is that poems referring to a specific event or person (such as 'Twin Screw-Set' or 'On John Maclean') but written at different times are out of sequence in a historical sense, but on the other hand are illustrative of continued influence or reflection or changed viewpoint. This occurs in only a few cases.

Sources are given in the notes. Most names and places are dealt with in the glossary. I have tried not to tamper with the texts, particularly with the pre-1900 poems: in general, spelling has not been modernised (except very occasionally for clarity) but obvious printing errors have been corrected; in the seventeenth and eighteenth-century verse, italics have generally been removed but initial capitals retained.

To quote again the now infamous passage from Alasdair Gray's novel *Lanark* (1981): 'If a city hasn't been used by an artist not even the inhabitants live there imaginatively . . . Imaginatively Glasgow exists as a music-hall song and a few bad novels.' This is deliberate exaggeration, of course, but I hope *Mungo's Tongues* has demonstrated that there is more to Glasgow verse over the last two hundred years or so than what 'I Belong to Glasgow' represents; especially so over the last thirty years with the development of a powerful body of Glasgow writing: the fiction of Gray himself, James Kelman, Janice Galloway, Jeff Torrington, Frederic Lindsay, A. L. Kennedy, Carl MacDougall and others; and the poetry of Edwin Morgan, Tom Leonard, Liz Lochhead, Stephen Mulrine, Stewart Conn, Robert Crawford and others. Of the poets, Philip Hobsbaum wrote: 'Their dialect voices are not masks assumed by skilled artists so much as a mode of dramatic speech. That speech has caused Glasgow to achieve recognition as an identity; it is now on the map, along with the Brontë country and Joyce's Dublin.' (*Glasgow Magazine* 3, 1983) Artists' motives, though, are not always so clear cut. Perhaps we have to be reminded that writers are individual human beings writing out of their own particular needs and concerns. That passage from *Lanark* goes on, and this bit does not usually get quoted, with the central character being asked, 'So you paint to give Glasgow a more imaginative life?' He answers, 'No. That's my excuse. I paint because I feel cheap and purposeless when I don't.'

I would suggest that the golden age of Glasgow poetry is over. The best of the Glasgow poets have long since demonstrated that their city constitutes real matter for writing and having done so are no longer in thrall to it. 'Glasgow

Poets': the best of them sufficiently deserve the noun as to make the adjective inadequate. They always had wider concerns, but their Glasgowness is now less self-conscious.

What of the poems of the future? Will they reflect the new image of Glasgow – the cleaner city, the centre of 'culture', the expanding service and entertainment industry? Glasgow will surely continue to provide sustenance for poetry, but what kind of poetry? Will it be a return to the eighteenth-century Augustan couplet –

> The Muse would sing, when Glasgow she surveys,
> But Glasgow's Beauty shall outlast her lays.

– as James Arbuckle wrote in 1721? Or will it be something new? Edwin Morgan recognises the difficulties: 'It's much harder,' he said in a recent interview, 'to write about central Glasgow today, which has had its face lifted, this doesn't give rise to feelings from which poems come. It may be more pleasant to walk about it and so on, very nice, very agreeable to look at, but it doesn't give rise to the kind of poems that people were writing . . . in the 1960s and 1970s. Perhaps if you're writing about a place and a city, writing about its problems, it's more productive than just writing a kind of PR job for the new Glasgow.' (Interview with Christopher Whyte, in Edwin Morgan, *Nothing Not Giving Messages*, 1990)

Obviously there are still problems in Glasgow – and poems to be written about them (see Cath Craig's 'Glasgow's Alive'). Edwin Morgan himself suggests the new generation of Glasgow poets is writing a more intellectual, sophisticated, political poetry, 'as if to emphasise the dramatic and challenging variousness of the city itself'. Perhaps there will be more science fiction poems, like Morgan's own 'Clydegrad'.

What I would like to see written is the kind of thing the Americans are not afraid to tackle: a long poem about Glasgow of the order of William Carlos Williams's *Paterson* (about his home city in New Jersey) – a poem which would bring together all of Glasgow, its history, its places, its people and their voices. Or a poem which would do for Glasgow what another American poet, Charles Reznikoff, did for America in his sequence *Testimony*, a verbal panorama of early twentieth-century American life, quarried from law reports of the several states – forgotten voices speaking again. The court records of Glasgow should provide a rich source for an urban epic.

Hamish Whyte
Glasgow
May 1993

Glasgow from the north-east, *c*.1672 (John Slezer, *Theatrum Scotiae*, 1693) MITCHELL LIBRARY

Glasgow from the south, *c*.1672 (John Slezer, *Theatrum Scotiae*, 1693) MITCHELL LIBRARY

Glasgua

Glasgua, tu socias inter caput exeris urbes,
  Et te nil ingens pulchrius orbis habet.
Sole sub occiduo Zephyri te temperat aura,
  Frigora nec brumae, nec Canis ora times.
Glotta latus cingens electro purior omni est,
  Hic regis imperio lintea mille tuo.
Pons iugat adversas operoso marmore ripas,
  Et tibi securum per vada praebet iter.
Aemula Phaeacum tua sunt pomaria sylvis,
  Ruraque Paestanis sunt tibi plena rosis.
Farra Ceres, armenta Pales, Thetis agmina gentis
  Squamigerae, nemorum dat tibi Diva feras.
Tecta nitent, ipsas et tangunt vertice nubes;
  Quo commendentur, plus tamen intus habent.
Templa domos superant, radiant haec marmore puro,
  Marmoris et pretium nobile vincit opus.
Non procul hinc Themidis se tollunt atria, patres
  Hic ubi purpureos dicere iura vides.
In medio residens sua pandit limina Phoebus,
  Hic cum Permesso Pegasis unda fluit.
Civibus ingentes animos Deus armiger, artes
  Nata Iovis, stabiles Iuno ministrat opes.
Moenia Dardanidum posuit Grynaeus Apollo,
  Et Deus aequoreis qui dominatur aquis.
Glasgua, te fausto struxerunt sidere Divi,
  Quot mare, quot tellus, quotquot et aether habet.

Arthur Johnston, *c*.1630

Glasgow

Glasgow to Thee thy Neighbouring Towns give place,
'Bove them thou lifts thine head with comely grace.
Scarce in the spatious Earth, can any see
A City that's more beautifull than thee.
Towards the setting Sun thou'rt built, and finds
The temperat breathings of the Western-Winds.
To thee the Winter colds not hurtfull are,
Nor scorching Heats of the Canicular.
More pure than Amber is the River Clyde,
Whose Gentle Streams do by thy Borders glyd;
And here a thousand Sail receive commands
To traffick for thee unto Forraign-Lands.
A Bridge of pollisht Ston, doth here vouchsafe
To Travellers o're Clyde a Passage safe.
Thyne Orchards full of fragrant Fruits and Buds
Come nothing short of the Corcyran Woods.
And blushing Roses grow into thy fields
In no less plenty than sweet Paestum yeelds.
Thy Pastures, Flocks, thy fertile Ground, the Corns,
Thy Waters, Fish, thy Fields the Woods adorns,
Thy Buildings high and glorious are; yet be
More fair within than they are outwardly.
Thy Houses by thy Temples are out done,
Thy glittering Temples of the fairest Stone:
And yet the Stones of them how ever fair,
The Workmanship exceeds which is more rare.
Not far from them the Place of Justice stands,
Where Senators do sit and give Commands.
In midst of thee APOLLO's Court is plac't,
With the resort of all the Muses grac't.
To Citizens in the Minerva Arts
Mars valour, Juno, stable Wealth impairts:
That Neptune and Apollo did (its said)
Troy's fam'd Walls rear, and their foundations laid.

But thee, O GLASGOW! we may justly deem
That all the Gods who have been in esteem,
Which in the Earth and Air and Ocean are,
Have joyn'd to build with a Propitious Star.

John Barclay, 1685

from Glotta: A Poem

Thro' flow'ry Vallies, and enamel'd Meads,
The hastening Flood at length to Glasgow speeds.
Its Northern Bank a lovely Green displays,
Whose e'ery Prospect fresh Delights conveys.
Alternate Shades of blowing Flow'rs we view
Of various Tincture, wash'd in fragrant Dew.
Here the shrill Larks their mattin Songs repeat,
The yielding Air the tender Strains dilate
As o'er the Surface of the Stream they glide;
And sweetly languish on the Silver Tide.
Here, when declining Sol extends the Shades,
Resort victorious Throngs of charming Maids.
Not fabled Paphos, or th' Arcadian Plain,
Could ever boast a brighter Virgin Train;
More gentle Looks, or Eyes more sparkling show,
Or Cheeks that with a livelier Crimson glow.
What envious Pow'r then first contriv'd, or made
That Foe to Beauty, and to Love, a Plaid?
Destruction seize the guilty Garb, that holds
Conceal'd such Charms in its malicious Folds.
Of this, O Thyrsis, could thy Strains unshrine,
Thy Saccharissa, how the Fair would shine!
Her bright Example would the Law impose,
And all the Green a Gallaxy disclose.

In Winter too, when hoary Frosts o'erspread,
The verdant Turf, and naked lay the Mead,
The vig'rous Youth commence the sportive War,
And arm'd with Lead, their jointed Clubs prepare;
The Timber Curve to Leathern Orbs apply,
Compact, Elastic, to pervade the Sky:
These to the distant Hole direct they drive;
They claim the Stakes who thither first arrive.
Intent his Ball the eager Gamester eyes,
His Muscles strains, and various Postures tries,
Th' impelling Blow to strike with greater Force,
And shape the motive Orb's projectile Course.
If with due Strength the weighty Engine fall,
Discharg'd obliquely, and impinge the Ball,
It winding mounts aloft, and sings in Air;
And wond'ring Crowds the Gamester's Skill declare.
But when some luckless wayward Stroke descends,
Whose Force the Ball in running quickly spends,
The Foes triumph, the Club is curs'd in vain;
Spectators scoff; and ev'n Allies complain.
Thus still Success is follow'd with Applause;
But ah! how few espouse a vanquish'd Cause!

The Muse would sing, when Glasgow she surveys,
But Glasgow's Beauty shall outlast her lays.
Tho' small in Compass, not the lest in Fame,
She boasts her lofty Tow'rs, and antient Name.
Rais'd eminent the sacred Pile appears,
Rev'rend with Age, but not impair'd by Years,
From holy Mungo nam'd; of daring Height,
And Antique Structure, awful to the Sight,
To Heav'n their Homage here the Living pay;
Here wait the Dead the Dawn of endless Day.
The neighbouring Rocks, and Mingled Graves encease
The silent Horrors of the sacred Place;
Bid Human-kind their latter End discern,
And living well, the Art of Dying learn.

James Arbuckle, 1721

John Highlandman's Remarks on the City of Glasgow

Her nainsel into Glasgow went,
   an erran there to see't,
And she never saw a ponnier town
   standing on her feet.

For a' the houses that be tere,
   was thicket wi' blue stanes;
And a stane ladder to gang up,
   no fa' to prack her banes.

I gang upon a staney road,
   a street they do him ca',
And when me seek the chapman's house,
   her name pe on the wa'.

I gang to seek a snish tamback,
   and standing at the corse,
And tere I see a dead man,
   was riding on a horse,

And O he pe a poor man,
   and no hae mony clease,
Te brogues pe worn aff his feet,
   and me see a' his taes.

Te horse haud up his muckle fit
   for to gie me a shap,
And gaping wi' his great mouth
   to grip me by the tap.

He had a staff into his hand,
   to fight me an he cou'd,
But hersel pe rin awa' frae him,
   his horse pe unco proud.

But I pe rin around about,
   and stand about the guard,
Where I see the deil chap the hours,
   tan me grow unco feard.

Ohon! ohon! her nainsel said,
   and whare will me go rin!
For yonder pe the black man
   tat burns the fouks for sin;

I'll no pe stay nae langer tere,
   but fast I rin awa',
And see te man thrawing rapes
   aside the Broomie-law:

And O she pe a lang tedder,
   I speir'd what they'll do wi't?
He said, To hang te Highlandmen,
   for stealing o' their meat.

Hout, hersel's a honest shentleman,
   I never yet did steal;
But when I meet a muckle purse,
   I like her unco weel.

Tan fare-you-well, you saucy fellow,
   I fain your skin wou'd pay;
I came to your town the morn, but,
   an I'll gang out yesterday.

Tan I go to my quarter-house,
   the toor was unca bra',
For tere they had a cow's husband,
   was pricket on the wa'.

O tere we get a chapin ale,
  and tan we get a supper,
A filthy choud of chappet meat,
  boil'd among a butter.

It was a filthy dirty beef,
  his banes was like te horn:
She was a ca'f wanting the skin,
  before that she was born.

I gang awa' into the kirk,
  to hear a Lawland preach,
And mony a bonny sang they sing,
  tere books it did him teach.

And tere I saw a bonny mattam,
  wi' feathers on her weim,
I won'er an she be gaun to flee,
  or what be in her myn!

Another mattams follow her,
  wha's arse was round like cogs;
And clitter clatter cries her feet,
  she had on iron brogs.

And tere I saw another mattam,
  into a tarry seck,
And twa mans pe carry her
  wi' rapes about hims neck.

She pe sae fu' of vanity,
  as no gang on the grun,
But twa poor mans pe carry her
  in a barrow, cov'rt abune.

Some had a fish-tail to her mouth,
  and some pe had a bonnet,
Put my Jannet and Donal's wife,
  wad rather had a bannock.

Dougal Graham, *c*.1750

Trongate, *c*.1770 (Robert Paul)
MITCHELL LIBRARY

from Clyde: A Poem

As shines the moon among the heav'nly fires,
GLASGOW unrivall'd, lifts her lofty spires.
Her num'rous fleets to distant regions run
Beyond the rising or the setting sun;
And from her various coasts collected, draw
The costly spoils of rich America.
Or with the wealth of sultry Indies stow'd,
Return triumphant, thro' the wat'ry road.
CLYDE's ample bosom labours with the freight,
And deeply groans below the precious weight.
For Commerce, glorious with her golden crown,
Has mark'd fair GLASGOW for her fav'rite town.
She makes her sumptuous edifices thrive,
And merchants rich in princely splendor live.
Extends her spacious streets on ev'ry side,
And rears her beauteous domes with stately pride,
And bids her very poor in palaces reside.
Where orphans learn to follow useful arts,
And well-taught morals sanctify their hearts.
But brightest far her stately temples rise,
Fit for his worship who spread out the skies.
One charms with beauty regular and chaste,
And elegance correct of Grecian taste;
The comely parts exact proportions know,
And to one whole by fit connections grow.
Another labours with the cumb'rous load
Of barb'rous ornaments profuse bestow'd;
Huge columns heave to an amazing height
The Gothic grandeur's vast unweildy weight.
The work immense the daring genius shows
Of that bold lawless age, in which it rose.
   More gay assemblies call the young and fair,
Fond to admire or be admired there.
At once the shining street moves all alive!

Chair urges chair, and chaises chaises drive.
The aukward Fop the shining Beau envies;
Olivia sickens at Belinda's eyes.
Artful Coquetts resistless glances wield,
And Rakes expect the coyest Prudes may yield.

*

Peace, babbling muse! thy heav'nly sisters frown;
Wear thy wild flowers, nor hope a nobler crown.
    Say, rather simply, in the crouded street,
How cart stops cart, and burdens burdens meet.
How hammer'd anvil, rattling frame, and loom;
The bell far soundings, and the thund'ring drum,
Rudely at once the tortur'd ear invade
With deaf'ning sounds tumultuously convey'd.
    Tho' oft the Muse to lone recesses flies;
And much she walks alone who would be wise:
Yet both the Sage and Poet are allow'd
To catch instruction in the busiest croud,
And those of both have ever brightest shone,
Who much convers'd, and often thought alone.
For in the pop'lous town we best may see
Of human life the strange variety.

*

Where royal NASSAU rides aloft in lead,
With laurel wreaths around his sacred head,
As in a common centre, are combin'd
Four spacious streets which stretch to ev'ry wind.
The wearied eye can scarce their length pursue,
The distant buildings less'ning on the view.
Along each beauteous street, on ev'ry side,
The stately structures rise with tow'ring pride.
Crown'd with superior, and majestic grace,
The fair Exchange displays her beauteous face.
    When Romish frauds our senses durst controul,
And kept in fetters bound the freeborn soul;
Her terrors GLASGOW early durst despise,
Embrac'd the truth, and fear'd not to be wise.
And when dire Tyranny his iron hand
Extended over a reluctant land:
Anxious, and trembling for her threat'ned laws,

GLASGOW with warmth espous'd their glorious cause;
Great NASSAU welcom'd; and have ever shone
The first in loyalty to BRUNSWICK's throne.
Nor will from just obedience depart,
While GEORGE's race can boast his patriot heart.
   Let Glasgow flourish, still in grandeur rise,
And rear her lofty fabrics to the skies;
And, parent STREAM, may still thy happy plains
Rejoice in Peace, and Plenty bless thy swains.

John Wilson, 1764

Port Glasgow, 1768 (Robert Paul) MITCHELL LIBRARY

The Cock-Sparrow and Goose, A Fable

A Goose there was in Glasgow town,
For beauty fam'd, a buxom lown,
Near which a sparrow had his hole,
A lech'rous bird, upon my soul.

He knew the goose was often tread
By ganders large, tho' she was wed,
And that her lust was of such sort,
She'd welcome ev'ry bird of sport.
This fierce cock-sparrow left his nest,
To tread the goose among the rest.
He hung his wings around her tail,
On which the goose did low her sail.
He bill'd about, ador'd her charms;
And then she gaggled forth her terms.
 'Go rob thy nest, my little cock,
And bring to me thy feather'd flock;
Then in my egg-bed thou mayst stray.
And drench in lust both night and day.
Thy parts, unequal form'd for mine
As a snuff-box to brewers nine;
Or as a trout in a mill–dam
I altogether in will cram;
Then lustily I'll shake my tail
'Till all thy sparrow-spirits fail.'
The cock agreed, then rais'd his crest,
And fillip'd round the gander's nest,
He perch'd into her lusty hole,
To see him top the goose was droll.
Like weather cock above a church,
Or a small bell o'er a large porch;
Sure such a sight was never seen.
May God preserve our king and queen.

THE MORAL

The dwarf and giant, black and white,
Base whores admit for perquisite.

James Wilson, 1771

Glasgow: a poem

Hail, GLASGOW! fam'd for ilka thing
That heart can wish or siller bring;
Lang may thy canty *musics* ring,
   Our sauls to chear;
And Plenty gar thy childer sing,
   Frae year to year:

Within the tinkling o' thy bells,
Wow, Sirs, how mony a thousand dwells!
– Where they get bread they ken themsels,
   But I'll declare,
They're ay weil clad in gude bein shells,
   And fat and fair.

If ye've a knacky son or twa,
To Glasgow College send them a';
Whare, for the gospel, or the law,
   Or classic lair,
Ye'll find few places hereawa'
   That can compare:

There they may learn, for sma' propine,
Physician, Lawyer, or Divine:
– The gem that's buried in the mine
   Is polish'd here,
Till a' its hidden beauties shine,
   And sparkle clear. –

In ilka house, frae man to boy,
A' hands in GLASGOW find employ:
E'en maidens mild, wi' meikle joy,
   Flow'r lawn and gauze,
Or clip wi' care the silken-soy,
   For Lady's braws.

Foulis Academy of the Fine Arts, *c*.1760 (from a drawing by David Allan) MITCHELL
LIBRARY

Look thro’ the town; – the houses here
Like royal palaces appear!
A’ things the face o’ gladness wear, –
   The markets thrang, –
Bus’ness is brisk, – and a’s asteer
   The streets alang.

’Tween ane and twa, wi’ gawsy air,
The MERCHANTS to the Cross repair;
And tho’ they shine like Nabobs there,
   Yet, weil I wat,
Commerce engages a’ their care,
   And a’ their chat:

Thir wylie birkies trade to a’
The Indies and America;

Whate'er can mak' ae penny twa,
    Or raise their pride,
Is wafted to the Broomielaw,
    On bony Clyde.

Yet, after a', shou'd burghers fail,
And fickle Fortune turn the scale;
Tho' a' be lost in some hard gale,
    Or rocky shore,
The Merchant's House maks a' things hale
    As heretofore.

– O Sirs! within but little space,
This GLASGOW's turn'd an unko place!
Here Piety, in native grace,
    Abounds in store;
And Beauty's saft enchanting face,
    Wi' gowd galore.

Whae'er has daner'd out at e'en,
And seen the sights that I hae seen!
For strappan Ladies, tight and clean,
    May safely tell
That, search the kintry, *Glasgow green*
    Will bear the *belle*:

There ye may find, beyond compare,
The bluiming rose, and lily fair;
The killing smile, bewitching air,
    The virt'ous mind,
And a' that Bards hae fancy'd rare
    In woman kind.

But what avails't to you or me
How bony, gude, or rich they be?
– Shou'd ane attempt, wi' langing eie,
    To mak' his maen,
They'd, scornfu', thraw their heads a-jee,
    Nor ease his pain.

If ony simple Lover chuse
In humble verse his joe to ruise,
The eident *Porters* ne'er refuse,
   For little siller,
To bear the firstlings o' his muse,
    Wi' caution, till her.

But waesuck for the *Chairmen* now,
Wha ne'er to a day's wark dught bow;
Sair will her lazy *nainsel* rue,
   Wi' heavy granes,
That e'er our streets were lin'd anew
   Wi' gude plane stanes:

Whan Writer lads, or Poets bare,
Frae Ball or Play set hame their Fair,
Their lugs'll no be deav'd nae mair
   (When pursie's tuim)
Wi' '*Bony Lady, shuse a shair!*
   Ye'll fyle ye're shuin.'

– O GLASGOW! may thy bairns ay nap
In smiling Plenty's gowden lap;
And tho' their daddies kiss the cap,
   And bend the bicker,
On their auld pows may blessings drap,
   Ay thick and thicker.

John Mayne, 1783

Glasgow from the south-west, *c.*1761
MITCHELL LIBRARY

36

Lunardi's Second Flight from Glasgow Described

The hardy seaman, when ashore,
Forgets the dangers of the main;
Nor fears the billow's loudest roar;
But mends his sheets and sails again.

Soon as Lunardi did arrive,
He wrote his friends he was alive,
And was to tak a second flight,
And sweem it easy in their sight.
Crowds came and saw what cou'd be seen,
And there was sport enough, I ween.
    He took his seat, got cruising orders,
To sail and land on Cam'sie borders.
He then mov'd up, but something held him,
Up gaed his heels and nearly fell'd him.
What means this stop? he cry'd, and swore,
When frae below some ga'e a roar,
There's naething stops you, in the least,
Only your net has caught a priest.
They cut the rope, down fell mess John,
And landed in a dirty lone.
The coast thus clear, he flew straight North,
And bent his course towards the Forth;
O'er Glasgow college steeple flew,
And then we had a pleasant view;
But when our eye had tint the sight,
It wore towards the edge of night.
When he was straight o'er Cam'sie Fells,
He then began to crowd his sails;
But here he met what made him stare,
Another brother of the air,

Wha made him light and tak a chair.
Some hands were got, and down he came,
His ni'bour help't him to a dram;
He got his vessel safely moor'd,
Then took a chaise, and in they stowr'd
To Glasgow, as the vulgar say,
And baith appear that night at play,
And got a ruff frae a' the house,
That made the billies unco crouse.

   Here we may spy wi' half an eye,
That a' Lunardi's dinna flie:
For mony a braw balloon we see,
          Baith gash and saucy,
Until their noddle twin them ree,
          And kiss the causey.
That gamester's wise that saves his stakes,
Baith for his ain and ni'bours' sakes;
For when his vessel bursts or breaks,
          Then down he'll come,
And then he's sure to get his pakes,
          When on his bum.

Robert Galloway, 1785

From Vincent Lunardi, *An Account of*
Five Aerial Voyages in Scotland, 1786
MITCHELL LIBRARY

Glasgow Reviewed and Contrasted

Ae winter night, impell'd by strong desire,
I took my wauking stick, and left my fire,
With nae design to enter house or hauld,
Until again I landed in my fauld.

   Up Glasgow streets I gaed, and they were clean,
For neither man nor beast was to be seen;
The shops were shut, and ev'ry thing was still;
For it was wearing near the hour of twel'.
The moon shone clear, the stars all seem'd to vie
Which cou'd excel in so serene a sky.
My thoughts recoil'd, by viewing such a plan;
I then thought on the vanity of man.

   What then is man! no more nor less than dust;
He laughs a while, and then returns he must,
And give account, how he his time has us'd,
To mend his talent, or his part abus'd:
An awful reck'ning this, to those who spoil
The best of talents, and the precious oil
That lavish Nature does on them bestow,
To worst of purposes do often throw.

   Thus meditating, still I wander'd on,
Until I came just hard by Glasgow Tron.
I heard a drunken blunderer afar,
And to escape his din, I step'd ajar
Below the pillars, then I stood fu' snug,
Till he advanc'd, not ten yards frae my lug.
With bacchanalian stride, he took his stand,
And, with a voice like trumpet, gave command.

   Fair Glasgow, now, step forth and make your claim,
For, 'mongst the first of cities stands your name;

Sing forth your beauties, hitherto untold,
Your outside painted, and your inside gold.
Your spacious streets, so regular in form,
Your stately fabrics, fit to stand a storm:
Your state to paint, night hardly gives me time,
But for to try't will scarce be deem'd a crime:
Her form is oval, spreading with her wings;
Or, as a balance, when it equal hings.
Five crosses she contains, which make her vie
With most of modern towns beneath the sky:
Saint Mungo's kirk stands high, from East to West,
And of a' Scotland's choirs it looks the best;
Two stately spires it bears, in one a bell,
For bulk and costly wark it does excel;
Three places here for worship, in repair,
And many a decent prelate has been there:
A mile it measures round, in ev'ry square;
So this must be a decent house of pray'r.

Montrose's lodging does our notice claim,
And shows a taste, still worthy of the name.
Its situation does command a view,
Envy'd by all, and but excell'd by few.
Here gallant Graham did rest himself a while,
When he set free the king of Britain's Isle:
When Cromwell and his corps push'd all before him,
He, at Kilsyth, did push about the jorum;
He then, at Glasgow, set the pris'ners free,
Likewise to Edinburgh granted liberty.

The College next, I think, commands respect,
The place of learning we must ne'er neglect:
Two stately squares it shows, with halls all round;
Where youths are taught in learning most profound,
To fill the Pulpit, or the Bench, or Bar,
To make them councils for peace or war.
Here come the Nation's hopes from ev'ry quarter,
And do their cash and time for education barter.

Eleven parishes this city does contain,
And full as many chapels here remain
Of different opinions; and, what is odd,
The same communion, and most holy God
Is worshipped, seemingly with fervent zeal;
And no man speaks against the public weal:
All this is gain'd by act of toleration
Which certainly is good, if kept in moderation.
Three miles the city measures, square and square,
And many a handsome fabric sure is there.
The plan is near compleat, but only one,
And that is taking down the lump of stone
That formerly did bear the name of Glasgow Tron.

The story ended, then we heard a voice,
The Bacchanal and I both trembl'd at the noise.
A spectre then we saw, of antient form,
Its body huge, its countenance a storm;
Upon the nether battlements it stood,
And thus address'd its brother craft aloud.

Stay, blund'ring mortal, stay until I tell
What I have seen, since I sat by this bell:
Twa hunder year and mair I've kept this ground,
And great's the alteration all around;
For then the town was sma', below the hill,
Tho' now, you ev'ry creek and corner fill
With streets, and wynds, and lanes, and noble structures,
That show a taste, just like their wise conductors:
What now are palaces, were only then
Just warm thatch houses, fit for honest men,
Who with their frugal wives cou'd rear a breed;
Bot what they spun themselves they nought did need:
A buffin on a woman's head then was
Thought far superior to the best of gauze,
A mankie gown, of our ain kintra growth,
Did mak them very braw, and unco couth,
A tartan plaid, pinn'd round their shoulders tight,
Did mak them ay fu' trim, and perfect right;
A leather shoe they wore, with silver pin,

Of hameward make, and digg'd at Menstra Green.
As for the man, he wore a gude kelt coat,
Which wind, nor rain, nor sun, could scarcely blot;
The plaiding hose he wore, and bannet blue,
When they grew auld, he then gat others new;
But yet this homely race, they minded trade,
In frugal honesty they fortunes made,
That did not dwindle thro' amang their hands,
But to their heirs left houses, cash, and lands;
They squar'd by conscience, and by hands did strive;
This was the best, and surest way to thrive;
But now these honest men have fill'd their urn,
And things, in course, have ta'en another turn;
For riches then were got by slow degrees,
Now handsome fortunes are procur'd with ease:
Send but a speaking booby into town,
With fifty pounds or so, to set him down;
In less than seven years he'll build a street,
Wou'd hurt an Irish lord for to repeat;
But be not proud of all these buildings fair,
And stately lands, that do ly here and there:
Where is rich Babylon, so fam'd of old,
With gates of brass, and bars of massy gold?
The place, unnotic'd now, can scarce be told.

Robert Galloway, 1788

Foulis Academy Exhibition,
College Courtyard, *c*.1760
MITCHELL LIBRARY

Kelvin Aqueduct, 1798 (R. Scott) MITCHELL LIBRARY

Verses on Viewing the Aqueduct Bridge, etc. Over Kelvin, near Glasgow

Along which the Navigation of the Great Canal *passes*

If Architecture's pride in modern time,
Can raise the thought from sordid to sublime,
Thee KELVIN BRIDGE, can sure that merit claim,
Thy structure stands unrivall'd yet in fame.

O'er thy huge pile, the eye transported strays,
From base to top, from summit unto base;
Nor more thy form strikes the astonish'd sight,
Than thy vast use the mind with sweet delight;

43

Below thee, Kelvin steals along her bed,
While Navigation sleeps upon thy head;
By thee, assisted, o'er th' abyss so wide,
The sons of traffic in procession ride;
From sea to sea they ply, from shore to shore,
And o'er thy shoulders waft their pond'rous store,
While trade increases, by thine aid supply'd,
And boasts a course which Nature had deny'd.

Tho' spiteful KELVIN threatened to divide
Forth's tumbling flood from joining with the Clyde,
Thy rising form, majestic, interpos'd,
Strode o'er the vale, and the wide gap was clos'd.

To vanquish Nature's local spite the more,
The trusty Locks retain their liquid store;
Which, from the height, by gradual steps, descend,
Till, on thy top the short liv'd torrents end.

How grand the view, when, from the hollow vale,
The eye, delighted, sees the coming sail;
With steady pace, her middle region ply,
And, on thy summit, hang 'twixt earth and sky:

Nor finish here, the wonder and amaze,
Which still must strike the curious stranger's gaze,
As they their course, from West to East, explore,
Or, from the East, desire the Western shore,
The curious Lock, obedient to the pin,
Swells, or contracts, her liquid flood within;
When the still barge hangs pendent on the brink,
Thy contents lessen with a gradual sink,
While thy huge gates, with wide expansion show,
A safe progression to the next below;
When the reverse, the rising water swells,
And that above, its empty neighbour fills;
While the proud barge, in elevation swims,
And, with slow motion, up the summit climbs,
So, having gain'd her course she onward bends,
Till in Forth's stream the Navigation ends.

Thus, all the features of this vast design,
In one great cause, their mutual efforts join,
While thy huge Fabric, tow'rs above the rest,
And stands the MONARCH of the Group confess'd.

Anonymous, 1796

Rab and Will, or the Twa Weavers

A True Tale

Hot-pyes and swats
Make weavers wits;
Gills, infidels and democrats.

Twa Calton swabs, ae afternoon,
Half fou, forgather'd i' the town,
A gill was instantly propos'd –
In lucky J*p's a' night they bous'd;
    The mair we share,
    We'd ha'e the mair;
    Wee cutty stoups are wylie ware.

They argu'd lang on church and state,
Decided fairly Europe's fate;
Priests, curates, bishops, popes, were tried,
The Holy Bible was denied;
Paine's Rights o' Man, and Age o' Reason,
Were held the best books in the nation;
Lords, Commons, ministers, they sat-on,
Pitt they regarded no' a button;
And thought it was dev'lish thing
They durstna speak against the King;
    But both agreed,
    His royal head
    Of nought but mortal clay was made.

They drank and roar'd till clear day-light
Had chac'd awa the shades o' night,
And through the broads, at every chink,
The morning sun began to blink;
 Their drowsy harns
 They claw'd by turns,
 And where they sat they made their burns.

They tried to walk, but wanted balance,
Their shouthers met between the hallans;
 Tak care, feet up,
 Cries lucky J*p, –
 She might have added, wyne, gee, hap.

Up the High-street they trudge as straight
As e'er ye saw a swallows flight,
Had common difficulties scar'd them,
The Bel – 'e Brae had surely ward them:
 Would they be beat!
 Na faith they yet,
 They'll rather try't on hauns and feet.

Pass'd Barrels Ha', the Alms-house clear'd,
Climb'd o'er the dike, through the Kirk-yard,
Cross'd the Mill-burn; the fir-park steep
They scrambled up, there fell asleep,
 Amang the trees –
 Dream'd o' bum-flees,
 Bag-pipes, wasp-bikes, and hives o' bees.

By this time it was hard on seven;
They lay and slept till near eleven;
The sun upon the High Kirk shone –
'Man Rab, (says Will,) do you see yon?
'The Kirk's no staunin' east and west!
'Some stormy night has gi'en't a cast;
'The sun's ay south at twelve o'clock –
'I counted twelve strike, ev'ry stroke;
'The shadow plainly proves it wrang –
'I wonder has't been that way lang;

46

'We'll through the burn and set it straight;'
'Are we that stout!' quo' Rab, an' laught,
   Syne gave his head
   A hearty screed,
   And damn'd an oath he'd tak the lead.

So belly-flaught down comes the twa,
Stript aff their coats, began to draw
An' tugg, each at a corner, swearan,
Ay now and then they fand it stearan;
   It gave sic rugs,
   Mice, cloks, and bugs,
   Thought 't would be down about their lugs.

Tobacco spittles routh they squirted,
Strain'd, stridl'd, squeez'd, pech'd, grain'd, and chirted;
At last they gave the desp'rate pull,
It rose two feet! – 'haud there' crys Will;
'Man strength wi' art is muckle worth,
'But ought that's o't ye're too far north' –
Far north – far south – quo' Rab, I'll sweare,
I sha'na put a haun til't mair;
It's nae wee lift; – wi' stress the froth
Wrung like soap-lather frae his mouth.

We'll drap it then, says Will, but what
The deuce has become o' my coat?
Some b—h frae the town head has stown't,
Or else we've set the kirk aboon't;
I've Deil anither, black or gray,
Nor yet kens whare ane's to come frae,
I would na, for a guinea note,
Be seen gaun hame without my coat;
Tho't yet should coast twa ruggs and draws
I'll hae the kirk back where it was: –
So manfully he til't again –
'Stop stop,' crys Rab, 'below yon stane
'For safety ye ha'e flung your coat,
'I see the tail o't keekan out.'

The tugg had lasted near an hour,
The twa their pith sat stumpan o'er,
Upon a grave, (their brains still bizzan)
The steeple bell twang'd out a dizan;
Our sons o' Samson glour'd at ither –
And to this day are in a swither
Which had been gleed, the steeple bell,
The sun, the kirk, or – Rab an' Will.

George McIndoe, 1805

Song: The Fair

Air – *Sandy o'er the Lee*

O Jenny thou's my joy and care,
   A dainty lass, and leal;
Come, gang wi' me to Glasgow fair,
   And le'e the spinning wheel?
O Johnnie lad, I darena gang,
   I'll no' gae wi' thee there:
My minny flytes baith loud and lang
   When I gae to the fair.

Hout, heed nae mair your minny's flyte,
   On me lay a' the blame;
I'll pledge my aith, before it's late,
   To see thee safely hame:
My daddy says 'Gae count your threads,
   And think on that nae mair:
For lasses tyne their maidenheads,
   When coming frae the fair.'

The tyning o' your maidenhead,
    There's little fear o' that;
To get a wean, I never try'd,
    Nor do I ken the gait;
Your minny's flyte, and daddy's frown,
    Ye needna mickle care;
I'll buy to you a braw new gown
    When we get to the fair.

So Jenny she's gane to the town
    For a' her parents said;
But weary-fa' the braw new gown,
    She tint her maidenhead:
And ay sinsyne she gaunts and grues,
    And ruggs, and tears her hair,
And greets, and cries, and sarely rues
    That ere she saw the fair.

Ye simple maids, be tenty a',
    When in ayont the stack;
For maidenheads, when ance awa,
    Can ne'er be gotten back;
What tho' ye're wi' a canny chiel,
    Sic like was Johnnie Blair;
And yet he play'd the vera Deil
    When coming frae the fair.

George McIndoe, 1805

49

Captain Paton

Captain Paton's Lament

Touch once more a sober measure, and let punch and tears be shed,
For a prince of good old fellows, that, alack a–day! is dead;
For a prince of worthy fellows, and a pretty man also,
That has left the Saltmarket in sorrow, grief, and wo.
   Oh! we ne'er shall see the like of Captain Paton no mo!

His waistcoat, coat, and breeches, were all cut off the same web,
Of a beautiful snuff-colour, or a modest genty drab;
The blue stripe in his stocking round his neat slim leg did go,
And his ruffles of the Cambric fine they were whiter than the snow.
   Oh! we ne'er shall see the like of Captain Paton no mo!

His hair was curled in order, at the rising of the sun,
In comely rows and buckles smart that about his ears did run;
And before there was a toupée that some inches up did grow,
And behind there was a long queue that did o'er his shoulders flow.
    Oh! we ne'er shall see the like of Captain Paton no mo!

And whenever we foregathered, he took off his·wee three-cockit,
And he proffered you his snuff-box, which he drew from his side pocket,
And on Burdett or Bonaparte, he would make a remark or so,
And then along the plainstones like a provost he would go.
    Oh! we ne'er shall see the like of Captain Paton no mo!

In dirty days he picked well his footsteps with his rattan,
Oh! you ne'er could see the least speck on the shoes of Captain Paton;
And on entering the Coffee-room about *two*, all men did know,
They would see him with his Courier in the middle of the row.
    Oh! we ne'er shall see the like of Captain Paton no mo!

Now and then upon a Sunday he invited me to dine,
On a herring and a mutton-chop which his maid dressed very fine;
There was also a little Malmsey, and a bottle of Bourdeaux,
Which between me and the Captain passed nimbly to and fro.
    Oh! we ne'er shall take pot-luck with Captain Paton no mo!

Or if a bowl was mentioned, the Captain he would ring,
And bid Nelly run to the West-port, and a stoup of water bring;
Then would he mix the genuine stuff, as they made it long ago,
With limes that on his property in Trinidad did grow.
    Oh! we ne'er shall taste the like of Captain Paton's punch no mo!

And then all the time he would discourse so sensible and courteous,
Perhaps talking of last sermon he had heard from Dr Porteous,
Or some little bit of scandal about Mrs so and so,
Which he scarce could credit, having heard the *con* but not the *pro*.
    Oh! we ne'er shall hear the like of Captain Paton no mo!

Or when the candles were brought forth, and the night was fairly setting in,
He would tell some fine old stories about Minden-field or Dettingen –
How he fought with a French major, and despatched him at a blow,
While his blood ran out like water on the soft grass below.
    Oh! we ne'er shall hear the like of Captain Paton no mo!

But at last the Captain sickened and grew worse from day to day,
And all missed him in the Coffee-room from which now he stayed away;
On Sabbaths, too, the Wee Kirk made a melancholy show,
All for wanting of the presence of our venerable beau.
 Oh! we ne'er shall see the like of Captain Paton no mo!

And in spite of all that Cleghorn and Corkindale could do,
It was plain, from twenty symptoms that death was in his view;
So the Captain made his test'ment, and submitted to his foe,
And we layed him by the Rams-horn-kirk – 'tis the way we all must go.
 Oh! we ne'er shall see the like of Captain Paton no mo!

Join all in chorus, jolly boys, and let punch and tears be shed,
For this prince of good old fellows, that, alack a–day! is dead;
For this prince of worthy fellows, and a pretty man also,
That has left the Saltmarket in sorrow, grief, and wo!
 For it ne'er shall see the like of Captain Paton no mo!

J. G. Lockhart, 1819

Queer Folk at the Shaws

Who ne'er unto the Shaws has been
 Has surely missed a treat:
For wonders there are to be seen
 Which nothing else can beat.

The folks are green, it's oft been said,
 Of that you'll find no trace:
There's seasoned wood in every head,
 And brass in every face.

Look smart, and keep your eyes about,
   Their tricks will make you grin;
The Barrhead coach will take you out,
   The folks will take you in.

Jamie Blue (James McIndoe), *c*.1820

Glasgow

A Poem, in Six Cantos

CANTO FIRST

Oh! could my muse take wing, and soar as high
   As yon tall pile that's named the monument,
Whose quill-like point writes on the azure sky,
   When dipped in clouds that darken the firmament;
   Then would I try, in colours bright, to paint
The jocund wonders of that borough town,
   The scenes of mirth, the hours of gladness spent
Beneath its walls and lofty towers, that frown,
Threatening the passengers as if they'd tumble down.

Then, wake, my harp, my harp so long unstrung,
   Till o'er thy strings soft numbers steal along,
Like strain that Echo wakes with silver tongue,
   Responding sweet the chime of milk maid's song;
   Oh! let the tuneful cadence, loud and strong,
Rise like the sounds from thrilling fiddle strings
   That Aleck rubs, to charm the list'ning throng,
That gather round to hear him, as he sings
His own-made martial song, till street or alley rings.

But, where shall I begin? what busy street,
   Among that motley number, first describe?
See, where they stretch, tramp'd by a thousand feet,

Glasgow Green, 1828 (Joseph Swan) MITCHELL LIBRARY

A thousand feet of every clan and tribe –
All characters are here, the priest, the scribe,
The ballad-singer, and '*shoe-ties, shoe-ties*',
    Pedlar and huxter, merchantmen that bribe
And tempt with ware of every sort, while cries,
'*Haddies*' and '*herrings fresh*' reverberate to the skies.

Look to the west, behold the river Clyde
    Moving along like gorgeous eastern queen!
In homage, palaces and towers divide
    On either hand to let it pass between:
    From bank to bank, that blooms with vernal green,
The stately bridges span their shanky legs;
    While, near their battlements, great crowds are seen
Passing the organ-man, that sits, and begs;
While some are at the wherries, cheapening fish and eggs.

Here, palaces and temples strike with awe
    The gazers, that admire their turrets proud
In lengthened line toward the Broomielaw –

54

Here, tackled trim with swelling sail and shroud,
    From every shore, the freighted vessels crowd;
And there, like Etna, flaming fire and smoke,
    The bottle-house throws out a pitchy cloud,
That darkens the air, and dims Saint Enoch's clock,
While passengers, that breathe 't, are gasping, like to choke.

Lo, what a range of taverns, stretching far!
    With landscape signs to draw the ready sale –
The Boar-head, Crown and Anchor, where the tar
    And Bacchanalian quaff the foaming ale,
    The dry-parch'd sense, long thirsting, to regale
With liberal draughts, that soon intoxicate,
    And bid the jovial song and smutty tale
    Among the noisy crowd to circulate,
Till boisterous swaggerings drown the long and loud debate.

But, let us now return; for we have passed
    Some merry scenes of jocund mirth and fun:
The Broomielaw intended for the last,
    With it the muse her song has first begun;
    But work like this can seldom be undone,
Though much better (like some of Baillie Cleland's):
    But, now we leave the Clyde, and let it run
Away, with steam-boats, to the western Highlands,
To visit hills, and lochs, and sail about the islands.

Then, first and foremost, there's the Gallowgate –
    A street so long, 't would take a day and more,
Even though the rhymes were running at the rate
    Of coining, in a minute, two-three score:
    Then, in this canto, we shall pass it o'er,
And leave it; for, if once we would begin
    There is enough, in many a hole and bore,
To make an austere bigot laugh and grin;
For, oh, what scenes are there of levity and sin!

Then, to Stockwell, or Goosedubs, let us turn –
    Or rather to the Bridgegate, where warm tripe
Fumes like frank-incense from odorous urn,

Or curling smoke from charged tobacco pipe,
    Till hungry wights their chins begin to wipe,
Well satisfied their bellies, big and bluff,
    Do stretch and swell like mellons fully ripe,
Betokening sure that they have got enough —
For Allan, Clark, and Veitch keep fat and famous stuff.

Here, down in the long dark close, where cheerless hovel,
    In squalid wretchedness and misery, lend
No fitting theme for fashionable novel,
    Even though its brightest scenes Sir Walter penned,
    Impatiently, would high-born dame attend,
Though eloquence would lisp the humble tale
    Of want and penury, without a friend —
Or female beauty, blighted, wan and pale,
Shivering like tender flower, in winter's stormy gale.

But, let us now proceed, nor tarry long
    Among the joyless scenes of want and woe,
To interrupt the strain and merry song,
    That should, with warm and kindling raptures glow;
    Oh! smooth and gentle be its rapid flow,
Chiming in sweet accord to jocund sounds,
    That now proceed from street, to whence we go —
Ringing throughout Saltmarket's farthest bounds
Tumult and clamour loud, that every voice confounds.

Oh! is there one fair town, that jewels earth
    With street like this, so full of thoughtless glee;
Where more is done than revelings of mirth —
    At least 't is whispered so 'twixt you and me,
    Reader, you know such things ought not to be —
Though fame reports, long here such things have been;
    But, if the rigid, learned and wise agree,
It matters not to us, for things unseen
We leave untouched to the immaculate and clean.

'Tis eight o'clock, and now the Laigh-Kirk bell
    Has rung a summons loud, that all obey;
For see what crowds come forth, and who can tell

56

Whither and where these various beings stray?
  After the weary toils and cares of day,
The grim mechanic leaves his noisy loom;
  The spruce-dressed clerk, and haberdasher gay,
Upon the Trongate, dandy airs assume;
While manufacturer steps toward the coffeeroom.

Down every flag-paved street and dirty lane,
  The living, mingling inundation pours,
Swelling, like common sewer after rain –
  In summer day, when frequent thunder showers
  Saltmarket's broad and polished pavement scours;
Till, ever and anon, through long dark close,
  Where changehouse shines, to wile away the hours
Some merry wights their roads, bewildered, lose,
While crowds of idle tag-rags gather near the cross.

Now is the hour, when, circling round the table,
  To hear when liquor pots are foaming full,
The loud harangue, both eloquent and able,
  Adorned with flowers that politicians cull,
  To rouse, from lethargy and stupor dull,
The free-born Briton, listening half asleep;
  For drink and nonsense sheer his senses lull,
And scarce asunder can his eyelids keep,
Save but to quaff the ale from goblet wide and deep.

Loud voices swell from taverns, crowded throng
  With Bacch'nal revellers, a merry *core* –
The long, loud laugh, the spirit-stirring song
  Is heard amid the universal roar: –
  Shakespeare, the Boot, the Sun, and many more,
Famed through the city taverns of repute,
  Where rosy Bacchus pours luxuriant store,
The nectarous juice of ripe elysian fruit,
Fit drink for men to quaff, and gods to distribute.

'*A row, a row*', gets up – and what a noise
  Of deafening clamour, strokes, and police rattle!
Strumpets, pickpockets, thiefs and blackguard boys

Join in the dreadful fray, the bloody battle: –
'Mid shouts the police come – courageous cattle –

*

The hubbub swells along the crowded street –
    Hark, how the fiddle sounds to merry dance,
In lighted halls, where swift and nimble feet
    Trip quick along; for laughing maids advance,
    With rosy cheeks, and sparkling eyes that glance;
They thread the living maze, like zephyrs light,
    'They meet, they dart away, they wheel askance,'
And turn their agile forms from left to right,
While every bosom heaves with throbbings of delight.

And, oh! what shouts, and peals of laughter loud,
    And joyful voices, tuned to mirth and glee,
Are heard to swell along that busy crowd,
    That's now engaged in thoughtless revelry!
    In sooth, it was a goodly sight to see
The buxom lasses and the rustic swains
    Mixing in noisy revel, wild and free,
Tripping, at times, to fiddle's thrilling strains
That loud and louder swelled, till morning lights the plains.

Oh! look not with contempt on humble life,
    Ye rich and proud, that move in lofty sphere!
Ah! little do ye know the care and strife
    They have to struggle with; their toil's severe;
    'Tis fit they should have times of social cheer,
Relieved from tyranny's oppression who
    Would lift the finger, with contemptuous sneer,
And blame their folly? Ye have follies too,
Though hid and polished o'er from erring mortals' view.

W. B., 1823

Humours of Glasgow Fair

Sic *transit vanitas* mundi.

I sing the sports o' Glasgow Fair
  As they were ance transacted,
Since nae kin' bard, in colours rare,
  Has ever them depicted.
The task be mine, though rude the strains
  O' my plain hamespun ditty;
I'll heartily bestow sic pains
  On my braw native city,
          The pride o' day.

Now, every ane, rigged in his best,
  Seems really unco happy;
An' speedily sets out in quest
  O' a drap cheerin' nappy.
Tradesmen, in haste, fling by their tools;
  The Smith leaves his forehammer;
The Labourer his picks an' shools,
  To join the mirthfu' clamour
          An' fun this day.

Wi' bauns o' canty, daunerin' fock,
  Paradin' an' repassin';
Wi' fiddlers, singers, in each neuk;
  Wi' laddin' an' wi' lassin';
Ye'll no get easy through the streets,
  Whan a' move on thegither;
But every body, that ane meets,
  Is knockin' on the ither,
          Thump, thump this day.

What constant gales o' yellin' soun'
  Are dashin' on the ear!
For out an' in, through a' the town,
  Focks ramp, an' roar, an' jeer.

Glasgow Fair, 1825 (Glasgow Looking Glass) MITCHELL LIBRARY

There's New'rday time, an' King's birth-day –
    But it will tak' them a'
To cope wi' this blythe time o' play,
    For laughin' is the law
              That hauds this day.

Now, *Jockies* wi' their lasses, thrang,
    Are makin' ordinations,
Whaur they will meet ere it be lang,
    After some recreations.
Fie, Jenny, dinna be sae blate
    As thrawart his intention,
For he kens it's nae deadly hate,
    But just a bit invention
            O' you this day.

A lad, ca'd Bauldy McIntyre,
    Had a sweet smirkin' dearie,
Her dapplet cheeks his saul did fire,

Love's darts shone in her clear e'e:
The youngsters took a wisp o' strae,
   An' hook'd it to her gown,
Then gaed a loud an' blythe hurra, –
   She ran aff wi' her clown
            Post-haste this day.

Now, couples ither couples meet,
   In mony a swaggerin' core;
Each lad performs some amorous feat
   Unkent to him afore:
He cannily slips his haun alang
   The outline o' her waist,
An' cadgily awa they gang –
   A kiss is quite a feast
            Worth gowd this day.

The lover now maun buy his lass
   Something to *haud her fair*,
For nits an' sweeties, as you pass,
   Are temptin' fock to wair.
A pun o' raisins, guid an' sweet,
   Made Rab's lass stick like glue;
She roosed him for this unco treat,
   Swoor she'd be kin' an' true
            To him this day.

But some proud, self-conceited queans,
   Pretendin' to be fickle,
Canna be won without new preens
   An' ornamental tackle:
While ithers, every inch as braw,
   Accept an humbler token,
An', quite contentet, jog awa
   To get sma yill to sloken
            Their drouth this day.

What a queer motley crowd hae met
   To see thae rarie-shows! –
The gallant chiel pays for his pet,

An' in wi' her he goes.
Sawney, wha had a soup o' drink,
   In climbin' up the trap,
Mistook a stap, fell owre the brink,
   An' got a fearfu' rap
              On his croun this day.

Hear, hear! what a discordant din
   Wi' trumpets, cymbals, drums!
The warnin' cry, o' 'just begin',
   From every showman comes:
'Haste, tumble in – no time lose –
   Fun ridin' upon fun –
See an' believe, without excuse –
   Such feats were never done
              Before this day.'

'There's Punch, an' cockulorum tricks –
   Ingenious machinery –
Dwarfs – Giants, measurin' seven feet six –
   The wild beasts' Menagerie –
The manly-lookin', o'ergrown Child,
   A wonder o' the age,
For strikin' features, visage mild,
   The boast o' History's page
              In any day.'

Unparalelled Equestrian feats –
   The little Horse o' knowledge,
Whose wit surprise an' mirth creates,
   Though not bred in a college;
The greatest rascal *he'll* point out,
   Or him wha hugs the lasses –
The beast rins twa-three times about,
   Then to his Master passes
            As *him* this day.

Commotion's risin' in the croud –
   'A ring, a ring!' they're bawlin';
If ony venture in 't, I dread,

They'll get a serious maulin'.
A rogue shoved in a kintra lad –
    'They dang him through the mill,'
Frae side to side, wi' mony a daud,
    Till he had got his fill
                O' dings this day.

But Willie Black, a senseless coof,
    Stared wi' a wylart glowr
To see his frien' thus dashed aloof
    Amid thick gusts o' stour;
So straight he rins, an' cries 'Fair play' –
    A thief gied him a twitch;
An' Willie, whan he turned that way,
    Fand he had lost baith watch
                An' chain this day.

Look, yonder is *a right brown hat*,
    I'm sure he is a Barney;
They rin to 'crown him' for a Pat
    That's travelled frae Killarney;
The 'SHIBBOLETH' has scarce been wrung
    Out o' the unwillin' cout,
Whan his hat in the air is flung,
    An' fa's wi' the *croun* out
                Dressed trim this day.

Here gamblin' knaves are carryin' on
    Their *never-failin'* tricks –
The box is jumled, dice are thrown,
    'Above six or below six?'
'Come, turn the wheel of fortune round,
    My hearties!' ane is cryin';
Some throw the Roul-Poul on the ground,
    An' tentily are eyein'
                Ginge-bread this day.

'On A or B – on B or A,
    Clap down your *happence*, brother;
There's no *desavin* in this way,

The one wins off the other.' –
'Never venture, never win,
   Your luck in lottery try,
All prizes and no blanks put in;
   Books, tapes or jewellery
           You'll draw this day.'

A chiel cam up to attempt the dice,
   Wha thocht to get a prize,
Plumps doun his *tippencce* in a trice,
   An' casts the settlin' dies;
They countet them twice owre complete,
   An' *forty-five* was summ'd
They luket for't upon the *sheet* –
   But saw how he was humm'd –
           'Twas *nocht* this day.

There's Packmen ranged in twa-three tiers
   Exposing their hardware –
'Come, lassie, buy a pair o' shears,
   Or caimb to haud your hair.' –
'Come, master, buy a jocteleg
   That does for cuttin' a' things,
An' edges on't like razor gleg;
   Nae doubt but different braw things
           You need this day.' –

'I hae a stock as guid as ony
   Ye will find in this fair;
Gin ye want tea-spoons for your money,
   I'm ready here to sair;
See, what a bright an' hansome polish,
   A dozen ye can't buy snugger,
An' vera cheap, if you're not foolish –
   For tea will need no sugar
           Wi' such as they!'

Here Auctioners are brisk uphauden,
   The fineness o' their cloth –
Ane's, now an' then, a penny bodin,

'To knock it down he's loth':
But when he thinks he's mann'd his price,
   He audibly calls out
'The bargain's going, once, twice, thrice,
   Come hand the cash about
          Without delay.'

Recruitin' parties, wi' their drums,
   Frae every ither county,
Are makin' gowks gie up their looms
   An' tak the listen bounty. –
Oh, hon! oh, hon! the wee drap drink
   Has drown'd the thocht o' sorrow,
Their gilded graith, an yellow clink,
   Will darker seem to-morrow
          Than on this day.

Hail, changehouse! for a moment now
   I woo thy dusky shade,
Whar monie a drucken interview
   An' devilish plan is laid;
For never did Tartarean groves,
   Replete wi' dismal pain,
Exhibit mae uncouthly droves,
   Than does thy fell domain
          This throu'ther day.

There clouds o' smoke ascendin' up
   Wi' bursts o' hideous roarin –
Here Politicians o'er their cup
   The Statesmens' ways explorin –
A wranglin' Committee is seen
   Maltreatin' and blackguardin' –
An' red an' blue are some focks' een,
   That haena been concordin'
          Like friens this day.

Closeby are several Wabster chaps,
   Fu' cozie near the ingle,
Their constant an' effectual raps

Mak' stoups an' glasses jingle;
Some doitet an' deleerit wise
    Are cuttin' dreadfu capers –
Some blinkin' wi' their half shut eyes
    On Samuel Hunter's papers
                    Nod nod this day.

The anxious bairns are toddlin roun',
    An' yamering for their fathers;
But scarcely will ye hear *their* soun
    For hurricanes o' blethers.
When Johnnie Gill, thocht time to flit,
    Frae seasonin' his car
He stacher'd aften back an' forrit
    Then coup'd amang the glar
                    On his doup this day.

Twa buikish fools grew bleezin' hot
    Upon some controversy,
An' belch'd an' blutter'd without thocht
    O' sense or mutual mercy;
Frae spite an' wrath it gaed to clouts,
    To cursin' an' to kicks;
At last, to settle a' disputes,
    The Police by the necks
                    Heuk'd them this day.

Three-bawbee yill, wi' nappy mixt,
    Made weak wives unco heady;
But pies an' porter was the text
    Held too by stomachs needy;
Some eat an' drink till they war stuff'd
    An' fou as they cud pang,
But sickness soon the burden cuff'd,
    An' they discharged lang
                    Sour spouts this day.

A drouthy tradesman wi' his *rib*,
    Sat hav'ren owre their gill;
An praised its contents – ca'd for Tib,

To bring anither fill.
They drank themsels sae royal fou
   As scarce to ken each ither;
But cleekit fast, they brave it through,
   An manage hame thegither
             Full sea this day.

Now druckenness appeared *there*,
   In a' its various stages –
To hear focks snorin' on the chair,
   It future woe presages.
The rate that Tammie was gaun hame,
   He'd soon wear out his strength –
He swoor, he fear'd nor deils, nor dame,
   Nor spunkie, nor road's length,
             But its breadth this day.

Oh, Whisky! but *thy* maddenin' heat
   Has risen muckle spore;
Though poets hae ransack'd their wit
   To laud thee an' adore;
For every ane *thou* dost inspire,
   There is a thousand more
Driven, through the vehemence of *thy* fire,
   To beg, from door to door,
             Bread for the day.

Yonder's a House to which droves steal,
   Pipers an Fiddlers playin';
A single penny for a reel
   Is the price they are payin'.
Each lad has waled his sonsy dear,
   An' brings her by the han';
In couples now they a' appear,
   To harmonise the plan
            O' the dance this day.

The Fiddler scrapes some canty spring,
   Which quickly sets them movin';
Dexterity is now the thing

That each is fond of provin':
Wi' noisy skill they ply their feet,
    As through the reel they gang;
In thousand measures, slow an fleet,
    An' monie a tiresome bang,
                In style this day.

The lasses' faces wi' the stress
    Are reddenin' an' glowin';
Rab gat a smile frae his dear Jess,
    Wi' native spirits flowin',
Then he, enraptured wi' this bliss,
    Fa's on her pantin' bosom,
An' saftly tak's a balmy kiss,
    That in a flutter throws him,
                O' love this day.

Jock Tamson was a cunnin' loon,
    He tald his love by winks,
For, every time he danc'd a roun,
    He lent her some new blinks:
But fate had been resolved to thraw
    The neck o' his invention –
He lost his feet, an', by a fa',
    Drew down the hail attention
                On him this day.

Now evenin's sober grey draws near,
    Wise focks are drivin' hame,
But some daft gowks, devoid o' fear,
    To wait, think it nae blame.
The kintra lassie kilts her coat,
    An' draws her dearie till her –
Some are thrang tellin' a' they've got,
    Some countin' what's the siller
                They've spent this day.

As, when Rebellion, breakin' out,
    Uplifts her lawless head,
Spreadin' derangement in her route,

68

An' dark appalin' dread,
Movin' wi' the terrific force
   Of Ocean's unawed swell –
So sweepin' in their rapid course,
   Disturbances, pell mell,
            Commence this night.

Now packmen's booths, and sweetie stauns,
   Display a general ruin;
An' numerous are the ready hauns,
   While guids an' gear are strewin:
A desperate raggamuffin crew
   The Wheels of fortune tosses –
If to yoursel a frien' you're true,
   Tak through the nearest closses,
            An' hame this night.

Dead cats, an monie a glary clout,
   Are fleein' fast athort;
An' chiels an' hizzies dang about,
   Wha think it nae great sport;
But, though ane's laid upon his doup,
   He needna ope his mouth;
But, soon as he can scramble up,
   Repair whaur there is routh
            O space this night.

Rab Blair had better been at hame,
   Suppin' a cog o' brose –
A rascal hit him wi' a stane
   Upon the brig o's nose:
When he saw streams o' bluid rin down,
   He dreamed he had been fell'd;
Till some fock hammered in his crown,
   He was not *really kill'd*,
            But hurt this night.

An' Maggie gat her trig new bonnet
   Bespattered o'er wi glaur;
She ran an' threw a napkin on it

'Guid's mercy it's nae waur.'
The mob stood laughin' like to split
    At her sae sadly cow't –
A sharper heel'd her wi' his fit,
    She tumbled like a nowte
                Bang up this night.

Pate thocht himsel' a man o' might,
    An o'er fearned to be cowrin'
'To one vile mischievous wight
    Who spends his life devourin'.'
So fearlessly he squared and buffed
    Like a man no himsel';
To a' he did they pewed and puffed,
    Then pump'd the Bridgate well
                On him this night.

Now monie criple wi' a clour,
    An' hing their head for shame;
An' monie rue unto this hour
    That e'er they gaed frae hame:
But let them keep a' they hae got,
    An' mak o't what they can,
Misfortune couldna but allot,
    To headstrong fools who ran
                Ram stam this night.

But broken bones an' cutet pows,
    Are famous wark for Doctors;
An' castin' out, an raisin' rows
    Are savoury jobs for Proctors;
It's fairs, an tipplin' wi' their fun,
    That brings Changekeepers food; –
The proverbs true – ''Tis an ill wun
    That blaws naebody good'
                Or luck nae night.

The sun has strak up through the lift,
    Wi' his revivin' blink;
Now focks that hae been turned adrift,

Begin to wake an' think;
Groups hameward bent, are trudgin' fast
    In dull an fretfu' mood,
Mementoes of the scenes bypast
    Will last till Death intrude
              On them some morn.

Observateur, 1823

Verses

Composed while walking on Gadshill, on the North side of Glasgow

By Glasgow's enterprising race,
Changes daily still take place,
Where late were fields and gardens green,
Lofty tenements are seen,
Churches wide and steeples rise,
Pointing far into the skies.
Pleasant mansions round I see,
In elegant simplicity,
Where citizens of worth and note,
Have oft their anxious cares forgot –
Freed from the City's bustling noise,
They find repose in rural joys,
Yet, daily walk in minutes few
To Town, their business to pursue.
Huge Cotton-Mills, and many a place
Of Industry, the Suburbs grace –
Here, from the height as we look down,
Saint Rollox seems itself a town,
Environ'd with a stately wall,
Excepting where the smooth canal
Incloses well the Southern side,
By which their port is well supplied;
It forms a harbour large and long,

71

Port Dundas, 1828 (Joseph Swan) MITCHELL LIBRARY

Where navigating vessels throng –
More emblems of their Trade we see,
By barrels pil'd upon the quay –
Some Arts unknown to Greece and Rome
Of old – to high perfection come,
As Chemistry proficient here,
New triumphs wins from year to year –
Here funnels of majestic size,
Ascend, and mingle with the skies,
Tow'ring like spires of pop'lous town,
Of metropolitan renown;
They vent the smoke aloft in air,
For passing clouds away to bear:
The skilful Workmen here show forth
The Owners' unaffected worth,
By the just respect they show
To their commands, with grateful glow;
For always they delight to see
The comfort of each family,
And scatter wealth with purpose good,
To give the needy clothes and food,
Th' industrious aged poor to warm,
To give weak drooping Age a charm.

William Harriston, 1824

Saturday in Glasgow

Wide through the cloudless lift o' blue
The twilight bright advances,
Till owre the Shotts knowes, wet wi' dew,
   The sun effulgent glances:
The mountains' streams, gilt wi' his beams,
   Like silver, twinkle clear;
The birds o' sang, the woods amang,
   Salute the tunefu' ear
               Fu' sweet this morn.

On this fair scene the Muse, in pain,
   Throws back an e'e o' pity,
As down the brae I bouncin' ga'e
   To view famed Glasgow city;
Whare mist and reek, wi' darksome smeek,
   Defy the solar blaze;
Whase inmates pale may sair bewail
   The absence o' his rays
               Sae aft by day.

Frae a' the airts the sour milk carts,
   Bot custom or embargo,
Reel fast and thrang the roads alang,
   Fraught wi' their sinfu' cargo;
While mony a mouth, sair parch'd wi' drouth,
   Is waitin' their arrival,
That late yestreen had whisky'd been,
   And's needin' a revival
               O' health this day.

Now mony a stiff and spavet horse
   Toils 'neath the great coal-waggon,
Urged to exert its utmost force,
   Through terror o' a flaggin';

While some, mair skeich, wi' head fu' heich,
  Are prancin' trim and trig,
As at their heels bright glancin' reels
  The coach, landau, or gig,
          Superb this day.

The barracks' drum, wi' thund'rin' din,
  Swells through her echoin' regions,
And to parade, rude, swearin', rin
  Her boist'rous vassal legions:
Now down the street, to music sweet,
  Straucht for the Green they're airtin',
While schule-weans, keen to please their een,
  Are frae their beuks desertin'
          In droves this day:

Wi' gleamin' steel, wide owre the fiel',
  The weel-train'd ranks are spreadin';
While awkward squads, without cockades,
  Wi' ill-timed pace are treadin':
Here, washerwives, wi' ban'less tongues,
  'Mang freathin' graith are splashin';
There, servant lasses, stark and young,
  The stour frae carpets dashin',
          Like reek, this day.

Mark yon black gang, that daily thrang
  Beside the jail, their hame,
Wi' visage din, japann'd wi' sin,
  And void o' fear and shame!
While owre ilk motion, gleg as fire,
  The police lads are watchin',
And, as light-finger'd deeds transpire,
  Most dext'rously they're catchin'
          Ilk blade this day.

Now troopin' to the warehouse, thrang
  The wabsters skeichly bicker,
Some hopin' tap-room mirth ere lang,
  While some are far mair sicker;

The men, victorious, on the van,
    'Neath national burdens groanin';
The wives are tempted maist to ban,
    While dearth o' tea bemoanin'
              Right sair are they.

Hech! what a het'rogeneous scene,
    Wi' business and wi' folly;
Some 'neath misfortune's burden grain,
    While ithers rant fu' jolly.
Here skulks a chiel o' noble soul,
    Wi' empty pouches pinin',
There struts a weel-clad jobbernowl,
    Wha is on sirloins dinin'
              Profuse ilk day.

Wi' bloomin' cheek, and manners meek,
    Now lovely maids are seen
Neist tawdry bawds, the glaikit jades,
    Wi' drumlie lustfu' een.
'Neath pond'rous burdens porters grain,
    And sweat through stark oppression,
While stout gigantic tailors vain
    Dose at their slim profession,
              In ease, this day.

Now scavengers, wi' clawts and brooms,
    The streets are trimmin' tightly,
Whare sights less fair than fiel'-pea blooms
    Are there deposed nightly.
The barbers glib, wi' razors keen,
    Are beards and whiskers mawin';
And fill their fabs wi' cash fu' bien,
    Though blood they're aften drawin'
              Frae plouks this day.

Hark! the wild skraich o' fishwives' snell
    Rings echoin' up the closses;
And auctioneers, wi' wit right fell,
    Joke owre the dyvours' losses.

Here fiddlers strike the dulcet strings,
    By gapin' crowds surrounded,
And there a sair-maim'd sailor sings
    How he in war was wounded,
                Right loud, this day.

On this han' moves the solemn hearse
    And sable-clad procession,
Whare gloom, beyond the power o' verse
    To paint, hold full possession;
On that a chaise like lightning flies,
    Scarce frae tap-gallop stoppin',
Whase inmates, bound in love's soft ties,
    To Gretna-Green elopin'
                Are, fast, this day.

Wi' weavers and tambourers, thrang
    The warehouse lobby's fillin',
Wha shore to leave the Corks ere lang,
    Wi' scarce a single shillin'.
Some ware their mite wi' muckle mense,
    'Gaint neist week's wants providin';
While ithers, void o' savin' sense,
    Are State affairs decidin'
                Owre th' ale this day.

Thrang, thrang the taproom boxes grow;
    Ilk core for news is ca'in';
Some greedily a speldin' chow,
    Some cut-and-dry are blawin';
On argument some enter keen,
    And mark state errors primely;
And some, to physic aff the spleen,
    Swill down the drink, sublimely,
                In pints this day.

Hence starved and ragged wives and weans,
    In want's drear hovels pinin',
While husbands are, wi' frantic brains,
    In alehouse senates shinin':

Whare, spendin' cash, they drink and clash,
    And Britain's weelfare plan;
Till speechless gabs and empty fabs
    Break up the doilt divan,
              When drunk are they.

Waesucks! for Britain's frail state bark,
    That aft to leeward veers,
Were she to ride the tempest dark
    Mann'd by sic timoniers:
Though wi' misconduct aft her crew
    Ha'e been severely branded,
Yet han's like thir, fu' weel I trow,
    Had her completely stranded
              Lang ere this day.

The New Street like a beeskep bungs
    In riot-like condition,
Whare butchers, wi' unhallow'd tongues,
    For profit risk perdition:
Here ladies, wi' mercantile air,
    Amang the stands are clav'rin',
While servants' faces plain declare,
    They inly curse their hav'rin',
              Sae vain, this day.

Here struts a flunky, liv'ry-clad,
    Fraught wi' a noble roast;
There flytes a souter's wife, half-mad,
    Anent a sheep's pluck's cost:
Some wauchle hame wi' sirloins fat
    In baskets on their hainches,
While ithers cater for the pat
    Guid fresh cow-heel, or painches
              Fu' clean, this day.

This day the Briggate hand-me-downs
    Cleed mony strange riffrandies;
Poor, naked, scawt Hibernian louns
    Come forth equipp'd like dandies;

Wi' backs to braid-claith strangers quite,
    And hurdies to hale trews,
Nae wonder that they feel delight
    When struttin in *surtouts*,
                Right spree, this day.

Here too the kail-pat shops, sae bien,
    Are in a perfect bustle,
Whare lab'rin' chaps, wi' stomachs keen,
    For service strive and justle;
For soup and kail, and beef and ale,
    A' airts at ance they're cryin',
While lasses rin, amidst the din,
    To stop their mouths, a' fryin'
                Wi' heat this day.

Wersh waefu' gear he gets, wha here
    Dines when the pats are eekit;
Sma' toil will he ha'e pith to dree –
    Experience weel can speak it:
Half-hunger'd drabs, wi' tasteless gabs,
    Amang sic graith may slabber;
To me a treat, before sic meat,
    Beer-scones and bonny-clabber
                Would be ilk day.

Mark poverty, in countless forms,
    Frae door to door slow creepin';
Sae toss'd by bitter fortune's storms,
    Nae wonder that she's weepin'.
Some listen to her waefu' tale,
    And cheer her abject face;
Some, haughty and unfeelin', rail,
    Unmindfu' o' her case,
                Sae sad, this day.

Around the Poors' House, age and want
    United, thrang are must'rin';
Their bodies frail, and faces gaunt,
    Might quell youth's vogie blust'rin':

78

Hail! ye, o' heaven-expanded heart,
   Wha plann'd this institution,
And sae judiciously impart,
   Wi' weekly distribution,
           Supply this day.

Fast frae his heicht the sultry sun
   Down western skies is slidin',
While some for health, and some for fun,
   On Clyde steam-boats are glidin':
Here tars, wi' faces black as sweeps',
   Toil at the block and tackle;
And there the sharp tidewaiter keeps
   Accounts o' rum and treacle,
           Fu' sly, this day.

Blithe commerce here hauds a' a-steer,
   To beet the back and wame,
And lets us pree the gusty bree
   O' foreign lands at hame;
Here moors, weel stow'd, the herrin' yawl,
   Graced wi' a guid sprit cable,
'Langside o' whilk the fishwives brawl
   As a' the tongues o' Babel
           Were lowsed this day.

Fu' mony a bing o' cod and ling
   Lies here for sale right handy;
And barrels big, to let us swig
   Dutch gin and fell French brandy:
A' kinds o' food, and drink, and drugs,
   To fatten and to clean ye,
Ye'll get, that grow – I'll lay my lugs –
   'Tween Ailsa Craig and China,
           In rowth, ilk day.

Now nicht throws east her dusky wing,
   To rouse the thievish varlets,
And thrang frae a' the closses spring
   Great troops o' lustfu' harlots;

Some, late enlisted in the trade,
    Show beauty's fadin' roses;
While ithers, lang in lech'ry bred,
    Display sair flatten'd noses,
             At the lamps, this nicht.

But here the Muse maun draw the screen,
    For she recoils wi' scunner:
To paint the brothel's scenes obscene
    Would gar e'en Pagans won'er!
Here, revelling till morning dawn
    In odious dissipation,
They break the fetters o' comman',
    And laugh at stark damnation
             Baith nicht and day.

William Watt, *c.*1825

Lines

on Revisiting a Scottish River

And call they this Improvement? – to have changed,
My native Clyde, thy once romantic shore,
Where Nature's face is banish'd and estranged,
And heaven reflected in thy wave no more;
Whose banks, that sweeten'd May-day's breath before,
Lie sere and leafless now in summer's beam,
With sooty exhalations cover'd o'er;
And for the daisied green-sward, down thy stream
Unsightly brick-lanes smoke, and clanking engines gleam.

Speak not to me of swarms the scene sustains;
One heart free tasting Nature's breath and bloom
Is worth a thousand slaves to Mammon's gains.
But whither goes that wealth, and gladdening whom?

Broomielaw, 1834 (J. Scott)
MITCHELL LIBRARY

See, left but life enough and breathing-room
The hunger and the hope of life to feel,
Yon pale Mechanic bending o'er his loom,
And Childhood's self as at Ixion's wheel,
From morn till midnight task'd to earn its little meal.

Is this Improvement? – where the human breed
Degenerate as they swarm and overflow,
Till Toil grows cheaper than the trodden weed,
And man competes with man, like foe with foe,
Till Death, that thins them, scarce seems public woe?
Improvement! – smiles it in the poor man's eyes,
Or blooms it on the cheek of Labour? – No –
To gorge a few with Trade's precarious prize,
We banish rural life, and breathe unwholesome skies.

Nor call that evil slight; God has not given
This passion to the heart of man in vain,
For Earth's green face, th' untainted air of Heaven,
And all the bliss of Nature's rustic reign.
For not alone our frame imbibes a stain
From fœtid skies; the spirit's healthy pride
Fades in their gloom – And therefore I complain,
That thou no more through pastoral scenes shouldst glide,
My Wallace's own stream, and once romantic Clyde.

Thomas Campbell, 1827

'Know ye the town where the smoke and imprudence'

Know ye the town where the smoke and imprudence
Are emblems of deeds that are wrought in their clime:
Where the woes of the weavers and loves of the students
Now melt in vile whisky, now soar into rhyme?
Know ye the town where the tall chimnies shine –
Where the walls are all sable – the rum is divine;
Where the winds are oppressed with such smoky perfume,
That the gardens are guiltless of seeking to bloom;
Where the stuffs and the cotton are first of all fruit –
Where the voice of the night-walker never is mute –
Where the dirt of the streets and the clouds of the sky
In colour are equal, in blackness may vie,
And often the river is purple with dye?

C. M. P., 1830

Glasgow from the south-east, 1828 (Joseph Swan)
MITCHELL LIBRARY

82

Petition

Unto G— R— and A— H—, Esqrs., Managers at B—
Dye-works, the Petition of A— R—,

Humbly Sheweth,
That,
Tired of the Town, of the Saltmarket sick;
With pledging plagued and pestered to the quick;
And driven distracted by a desperate squad,
Whose clamorous clack would clatter meek men mad: –
Your humble suppliant, supplicating low,
Ventures to vent, in wailings wild, his woe;
Trusting you'll listen to his groaning grief,
And stretch a helping hand to his relief.

O dark and dreary be that doleful day,
When to this sink of sin seduced away,
He turned on blythesome B— his back:–
May that day in the Heavens be ever black,
When he exchanged the haunts of hearty men,
For a dark, dismal, dingy, dusty den;
Condemned to draw in draughts of putrid air,
And pine amidst anxiety and care,
While turning over Mammon's meanest coin,
Bronzed o'er with blubber, herring scales and brine;
Obliged each day and hour to undergo
The pain of hearing tales of want and woe,
So finely framed, with so much feeling told,
As would make misers give, nor grudge, their gold:
Compelled to handle every dirty rag,
Stript from the hide of every hateful hag,
And doomed each finer feeling to degrade,
By bullying every blackguard trull and jade,
Who hither comes her tawdry trash to pop,
That she may drink it at the next dram shop.

That your said suppliant sadly suffers sore,
From these said ills on ills, and many more,

Which, but to name, or even to think of, must
Make man's flesh creep with loathing and disgust.

　　　Now, may it therefore please you, Sirs, to list
To your Petitioner's sincere request,
And take his case into consideration,
To save him from this every day's damnation;
And into your employment take him back,
And he'll take any job however black,
Rather than stay in this detested place,
Cut off from all communion with his race,
(Or if it be the human race he sees,
Good God, it must be, sure, the very lees.)
He'll fire your furnaces, or weigh your coals,
Wheel barrows, riddle ashes, mend up holes,
Beat cloth, strip shades; in short, do any thing,
And your Petitioner will ever – sing.

Alexander Rodger, 1832

Sanct Mungo

Sanct Mungo wals ane famous sanct,
　　And ane cantye carle wals hee,
Hee drank o' ye Molendinar Burne,
　　Quhan bettere hee culdna prie;

Zit quhan hee culd gette strongere cheere,
　　Hee neuer wals wattere drye,
Bot dranke o' ye streame o' ye wimpland worme,
　　And loot ye burne rynne bye.

Sanct Mungo wals ane merry sanct,
　　And merrylye hee sang;

Quhaneuer hee liltit uppe hys sprynge,
   Ye very Firre Parke rang;

Both thoch hee weele culd lilt and synge,
   And mak' sweet melodye,
Hee chauntit aye ye bauldest straynes,
   Quhan prymed wi' barlye-bree.

Sanct Mungo wals ane godlye sanct,
   Farre-famed for godlye deedis,
And grete delyte hee daylye took
   Inn countand owre hys beadis;

Zit I, Sanct Mungo's youngeste sonne,
   Can count als welle als hee;
Bot ye beadis quilk I like best to count
   Are ye beadis o' barlye-bree.

Sanct Mungo wals ane jollie sanct:–
   Sa weele hee lykit gude zil,
Thatte quhyles hee staynede hys quhyte vesture,
   Wi' dribblands o' ye still;

Bot I, hys maist unwordye sonne,
   Haue gane als farre als hee,
For ance I tynd my garmente skirtis,
   Throuch lufe o' barlye-bree.

Alexander Rodger, 1832

'Yes, yon fair town'

Yes, yon fair town
May stand a ruin on the living earth!
Her domes of pleasure and her palaces,
Rayless, and roofless; and her obelisks
Breaking the silent atmosphere where life
No longer maketh echo. The proud marts
Where thousands met, the halls where splendour sat,
The long saloons where bright-eyed beauty led
The giddy dance, the stately theatres, where
The gaping throats of myriads roar'd applause,
And sent it round and round the ample walls
Like rolling thunder; and the countless homes,
The meek, the humble dwellings of the poor,
Where high-soul'd worth – the poverty, the pride
Of honest freemen – round their hearths of love
Rear'd children, Scotland's glory and her boast, –
All, all will stand forsaken, and the fox,
The grey wolf of the desert, make their den
Amid her shatter'd temples; from between
The rent and fallen pillars looking out,
With savage growl on the adventurous foot,
That dares disturb their loathsome majesty.
And snakes may cleave the long and rustling grass,
That clothes each spacious and deserted street;
The bittern from the Clyde, the dozing owl,
Join'd with his boon companion the lone wind,
Shriek forth their solemn melancholy songs,
Throughout the high majestic porticoes
Festoon'd with wild flowers:– nought of man be seen;
The crowds all gone, the dead hid in their graves,
And the wild scream of the high-soaring kite,
The curlew's mournful echo, as she springs
From the gigantic water-weeds, that choke
That tide where nations traffick'd, now be all

The hum that speaks existence, or at times
The distant shadow and the graceful path
Of some strong eagle journeying to the north,
High, high above the city, or the clouds,
Those only licensed wanderers through heaven,
Flinging their huge enormous shadows o'er
The twilight ocean of unnumber'd roofs,
That ridge on ridge, in awful stateliness,
Checker the solitary wastes of blue.

Dugald Moore, 1833

from The Weaver's Saturday

A Political Poem

In Clutha's peaceful vale, the summer night
   Is beautiful, and man enjoys repose.
On Glasgow streets the watchmen mark the flight
   Of circling hours, and call them at their close.
The rural villages around the queen
   Of cities darkling lie, all hushed and still;
The twinkling stars and lamps are dimly seen;
   The rolling mist ascends on Cathkin hill,
   And here and there a lark, his hymn begins to swell.
               *
The young mechanic, weary-worn with toil,
   Can best enjoy the luxury of sleep;
Nor wakeful tosses unrefreshed the while,
   But rests in slumber, gentle, calm and deep –
No fearful dream disturbs his active brain,
   The charming hours roll on, and still he lies
In pleasing apathy, of care and pain,
   Until the glorious dawn begins to rise,
   And then awakes refreshed, and to his labour hies.

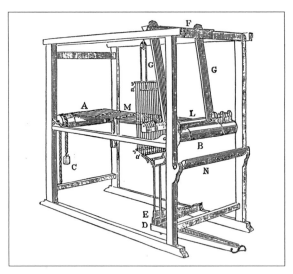

Loom, 1835 (*Book of Trades*, Glasgow) MITCHELL
LIBRARY

The sun is peeping o'er Saint Mungo's fane,
    And stern necessity from scanty sleep
Bids Robin Tamson ope his weary e'en,
    Else want and wae may gar his family weep.
Four helpless bairns his labour must sustain;
    Wee Tam, the infant, sucks his mother's breast;
Blythe Kate, the auldest, grown a sonsy queen,
    Can wind a pirn, and lull the bairn to rest,
    But skelping on the loan does often please her best.

*

To the loom-shop he wends his peaceful way,
    The rusty lock's withdrawn with little din;
His thrifty wife, with evening's glim'ring ray,
    Had wound the pirns to weave a dressing in;
But many a pirn he'll need, she kens fu' weel,
    Before he reach the waeroom door at noon;
Bids Katy hush wee Tam, and at her wheel
    She cowers, and winds the pirns with eerie croon,
    For morning flees away, and meikle maun be done.

The homely breakfast must be fast prepared –
    Hung o'er the fire the pot begins to boil,

And guid auld meal, in neivfu's quickly stirred,
    Makes healthy parritch, to sustain their toil.
Kate lifts the poker from the ingle nook,
    And dirls it gently on the auld deal floor;
Up Robin comes, and, weary-worn, doth look
    Full solemn at the grace o'er Scotland's fare,
    And wife and bairns beside him crack and take their share.

A toom meal barrel, and an empty pouch,
    Auld sair-worn clothes, and clouts frae neck to heel,
Bare-footed bairns, and wife wi' tattered mutch,
    Are cheerless pictures in a poor man's beil' –
The best of men are often most oppressed.
    Oppression, honest independence, chills –
And rouses indignation in the breast,
    And feeling hearts with reckless fury fills,
    That might be still serene, if less distressed with ills.

Hard is your fortune, nurslings of the loom –
    Cradled in sorrow, reared in joyless toil,
Stumbling and lost in dull commercial gloom,
    Uncheered by hope, your anguish to beguile –
No sun illumines the clouds that thicken round,
    Still blacker as you penetrate their gloom –
Sombre as midnight, dismal and profound
    As pandaemonium, is your wretched doom,
    And chained like galley slaves you ply the weary loom.

*

Poor Robin wends in silence to his wark,
    The shuttle skirls alang each silky thread;
In summer days he sits from dawn till dark,
    And yet his wages scarce supply his need.
The heddles dance, the lay comes clinking ben,
    The beam winds up the cloth before his breast,
And when he weaves a lang dreigh dressing in
    The brushes scud. He waves the breezy fan
    Aboon the clammy web, and dries it fast again.

At length the ling'ring keel appears in view,
    Roll'd on by bores, progressive to the fel;

Behind the shaft, he rumps it neatly through,
    Unwinds the cloth, and picks and folds it well,
Brushes his thread-bare claes, and dights his face,
    And trysts to meet his wife at Glasgow Cross,
And, heavy-laden, hastes with haflins race,
    For weel he kens there's little time to lose,
        The bell rings two just as he tramps the warehouse close.

In the gray lobby, he inquires his turn,
    Among poor weavers, grumbling at their ills;
Some curse taxation, some their rotten yarn,
    And some condemn steam-looms and cotton-mills.
Aye, one by one, they dwindle fast awa',
    'Tis Robin's turn, and now he stammers ben,
The petty foreman picks out ilka flaw,
    Keeks in the web-glass, counts, and keeks again,
        Flings ben the cloth, and Robin fidges unco fain.

The foreman was a weaver in his youth,
    Kens what it is to labour and be poor, –
But now to ape the master, he, forsooth,
    Must whiles display the tyrant, rage and swear,
Sometimes he crously cracks of auld langsyne,
    And vain, with self-complacency, will tell,
How men like him, in trade, made Glasgow shine,
    How, by his merit, he advanced himsel';
        But weel does Robin ken it's lies as false as hell.

A master wants a grieve to rule his work,
    He will select the man who suits him best,
A heartless hypocrite, a savage Turk,
    To rob his hirelings, trample the oppress'd,
As craft or selfishness inclines his mind.
    But workmen need not groan except they please;
Can petty masters thrive, unless mankind
    Shall toil for them, while they indulge in ease,
        And workmen, if united, may their labours cease?

And what could masters do, if all the men,
    Who toil for wages, but a month stand still?

Stocks, merchants, Britain would be bankrupt then,
   Wild anarchy destroy and rob at will;
And this can workmen do, whene'er they choose,
   By union, for the labour rests on them.
Why then to mitigate their wrongs refuse?
   The millions why to penury condemn?
   If British labour strike, where proud Britannia then?

Says Robin, 'Sir, I want a little weft;
   I'll need, I think, at least three spindles more,
When the web's woven, if there's any left,
   I'll ev'ry thread, with honesty restore;
The times are hard, I'll thank you for a *crown*;
   I'm in your debt, I do not like it well,
To the new web be pleased to mark it down;
   I hear you've put a *farthing* on the ell,
   I'm proud to say you have advanced it first yoursel.'

These little wants are settled without strife,
   The weft, the crown, the web, and *farthing* mair,
And then at Glasgow Cross he meets his wife;
   And gives her all his wealth, the *crown*, to ware,
Beside King William, where they oft have met.
   Her flich'ring bairns are clinging by her gown;
With solemn face she warns and counsels Kate,
   To guide wee Mary toddling through the town,
   For fear she may be stolen by some auld gypsy loun.

With gleesome heart he tells the happy news,
   Her bosom with delightful rapture burns,
And, with maternal providence, she buys
   A penny roll, and deals it to her bairns.
Wee Tammy slumbers at her yearning breast,
   Wee Bobby stachers at his daddy's feet,
And Kate and Mary, hand in hand compressed,
   At unco fairlies glow'ring on the street,
   Are proud to see their parents crack with friends they meet.

Now weavers wander thrang in Glasgow town,
   Some blythely cracking on the busy street,

Some toddling hame to weave the afternoon,
  And some with cash their greedy lairds to meet.
Some buy the *Argus*, *Lib'rator*, *Scots Times*,
  Some in a temp'rance tap-room, sit and whine,
A muslin bard recites his village rhymes,
  And in *Gazette* and *Chronicle* will shine,
  While he is doomed to rags – denied the means to dine.

Poor muslin bards, I embrace you all;
  The wayward muse may lead you often wrong,
But still you strike your lyres at nature's call,
  And patriotic frenzy swells your song.
Oft have I sat the warbling train among –
Blythe Rodger's muse, a bonny sonsy queen,
  In Scottish garb lilts canty, chaste, and braw;
O'er Tannahill the plaid of Burns is flung;
  Craig's humble grave will soon be clad with snaw,
  And Wilson's fame and dust are honoured far awa'.
                    *
The market's made, and Robin homeward turns,
  A homely basket dangling on his arm;
In Gallowgate he treats his wife and bairns;
  A wee drap ale their morals cannot harm.
To Tam's braw cellar briskly they gang ben,
  A strapping lad brings in the whisky stoup,
And crimpy cakes to make the *wee things* fend,
  Whose artless hearts with merry rapture loup,
  While daddy shares the cake, and bids them smack it up.
                    *
The weaver and his family take the road,
  Refreshed and happy, frisky, blythe wi' fun,
At sober eve they reach their sweet abode,
  And there the frying-pan begins to croon,
Clad with fresh herring landed from Lochfyne,
  Well spiced and sappy for a hungry gab,
The bonny tea-cups on the table shine;
  And Robin, on his chair, like any nab
  Beside his wife and bairns, brags o'er his promised web.

God's blessing sought with reverence, they begin,
  Nor fash with gentle ceremonious airs,

The happy children sit with merry din
  Around the table and partake their shares.
Then Robin hums the patriarchal grace,
  And thanks the Lord for all his mercies great,
Imploring him to guard the rising race
  From secret snares, that youthful life await,
  And aye prepared for death, their only certain fate.

The dressing pot's hung o'er the glowing fire,
  And cautious heated till it slowly boil,
And friendly shopmates kindly help to stir;
  And Robin, grateful for their gen'rous toil,
Tells glorious news, how commerce through the gloom,
  Blinks like a star on Britain's happy isle,
And muslin weavers, pining at the loom,
  Shall yet have some reward for weary toil;
  A *farthing* on the ell can make the weaver smile.

Each stirs awhile aboon the vivid lowe,
  And sweat is trickling down their beards like beads,
Scouring the lazy spurtle, doughtily,
  They often wipe their reeking, sweating heads;
To crown the scene, the scanty bawbees jingles;
  Each joins a penny, and maun ha'e a smack
Of barley bree, by Robin's cheery ingle,
  To chase 'cauld care awa' ', and welcome back
  Sweet blinks of auld langsyne, and gar him laugh and crack.

O, why does stern oppression crush the poor,
  And moral knowledge elevate their hearts?
Doom'd from a master labour to implore,
  And thank him for the mis'ry he imparts.
Ye petty tyrants, puff'd with puny pride,
  Why are your slaves at home in want and gloom?
Why do the poor in poverty abide?
  Philanthropy bewails your hopeless doom,
  Proud intellectual men, slaves of the wretched loom.

                              *
But I digress, and will resume my tale:
  I left the honest weavers unco happy,
The summer day is closed in Clutha's vale,

93

And the red sun is gone to take his nappy
Beneath our hemisphere, on ocean's breast,
    And now the Queen of night begins to glide,
On the blue sky she stamps her silver crest,
    The ev'ning star is twinkling by her side,
    Fair as a smiling child led by an eastern bride.

How fresh and charming in the summer night,
    By Clyde's delicious bank to steal alone
In pensive mood, beneath Diana's light,
    And all the stars but lovely Venus gone,
Or with the maid you love to sit unseen
    At Belvidere, beneath a flow'ring thorn,
Perfumed by odour of the fragrant bean,
    Or happily couch'd among the waving corn
    Twined in her glowing arms, till chased by dawning morn.

Sweet is the lover's walk at parting day –
    Sweet to the Christian smiles the Sabbath morn –
Sweet to devotion comes the hour to pray –
    Sweet to the mother's breast the child new-born –
Sweet is the Bible to the sound believer –
    Sweet is excitement when the mind is dull –
Sweet is cold water to a burning fever –
    Sweet to phrenologists the noble skull –
    But sweeter to the weaver is the *farthing* on the ell.

*

My tale is done – the weavers drink Guid-night,
    And toddle merry home, to wife and weans,
With independent hearts, exulting light,
    But weary of oppressive toils and pains;
And Robin breathes an evening prayer to God,
    For His protection down the vale of life,
To shield him from the fierce oppressor's rod,
    And guard sweet home from wild domestic strife,
    And make him meet in heaven his children and his wife.

Anonymous, 1838

94

Let Glasgow Flourish!

Air – *Cauld Kail*

Some sing of love, some sing of war,
And some their tales of pity,
But here's a wiser strain by far,
'Tis Clutha's noble city!
That place of commerce, wealth, and power
Which wit and genius nourish,
May still her Tree majestic tower –
Huzza! let Glasgow flourish!

For Clutha's famous city stands
In all-increasing splendour,
And daily do new-peopled lands
Their varied treasures send her!
She grows in science, wealth, and arts,
In beauty quite enchanting;–
In starry eyes, and glowing hearts,
And all that once was wanting.

And here's to you ye maidens fair;
Ye maidens chaste and pretty! –
Where'er ye are may ye declare
Love for your native city.
Then, sing with me her growing power,
Which wit and genius nourish –
May still her Tree majestic tower;
Huzza! let Glasgow flourish!

Andrew Park, 1842

Glasgow

I trod thy streets, proud city of the Clyde!
    Great mart of commerce! and on every hand
Were sights and sounds to trade alone allied,
    Yet fraught with dreams of many a distant land.
Thou art, – as cities from remotest time,
    Tyre, Sidon, Babylon, and all have been, –
A very world of wretchedness and crime;
    At once rich, poor, magnificent, and mean:
Still, there are human hearts within thy walls,
    So purified, so broadly stamped with 'Heaven',
That thou – 'tis known on high, whate'er befalls –
    Not wholly to idolatry art given;
And works of mercy have been done in thee,
That towns and nations might repent to see!

Mary Macarthur, 1842

St Rollox Lum's Address to its Brethren

Haud up your heads, ye stunted things,
Or gudesake get the len' o' wings,
An' soar aloft like me, where sings
        The cheery lark,
When frae its dewy bed it springs
        In some green park.

St Rollox Works (*Great Industries of Great Britain*) MITCHELL LIBRARY

My troth! your makers little knew
About stalk vents when they made you,
Or they wad ne'er ha'e made a crew
    Sae void o' graces,
As day by day black reek to spew
    In ladies' faces.

I see that frae the morning's dawn
Till ev'ning has her curtain drawn,
Ye spread your vapours o'er the lan'
    Sae thick, in faith!
That those who pass you aft maun stan
    An' gasp for breath.

Now just turn up your een an' see
The vapour as it rolls frae me,
An' ye'll confess that men maun flee
    In a balloon,
Ere they amang my reek can be,
    Morn, e'en, or noon.

Amang the clouds I keep my head,
And on their curling gloom I shed
My vapours that with them are spread
          O'er land an' sea,
While yours, ye are sae lowly bred,
          Scarce reach my knee.

The steeples that aroun' you rise,
Nae doubt, ance boasted o' their size,
But fient a ane o' them now tries
          To lift an e'e,
Or speak ae word about the skies
          Since they saw me.

But then, the dwarfs their bells will ring,
On Sabbath days, a crowd to bring,
To hear some college-bred bit thing
          Prove to a hair,
The nature o' creation's king,
          By dint o' lair.

Or if a battle has been gained,
And earth by human carnage stained,
Their bells, ye ken, are never hained,
          But loudly tell,
How weel vain men their powers have strained
          To mimic h–ll.

For nobler purposes was I
Exalted mid-way to the sky,
Than mak' a din when fools wad cry
          A battle's won,
Or sic a ane in station high
          Has had a son.

In the great cause of Art I rose,
And Art in me a wonder shows,
Such as is never seen in those
          They steeples ca',
Things gude for naething, I suppose,
          But mak' streets braw.

They tell us that in days o' yore,
Ane Cheops Egypt's sceptre bore,
Wha built a pyramid, a score
        O' feet an' mair,
Aboon where I the skies explore,
        Sae bland an' fair.

And proudly still the stately pile
Heaves high its head aboon auld Nile;
And from each continent and isle
        Will Cheops' tomb,
For ages yet, mankind beguile
        Frae friends an' home.

But after a', wha wad compare
A pyramid to them that share,
Like me, the toils that mankind bear
        Frae morn till e'en,
Save sumphs, wha think that naething's rare
        That's daily seen?

Beneath my shade Industry plies
Her eager hands to reach the prize,
That gained, adds lustre to the eyes
        Of old and young,
And bids hope's cheering accents rise
        Frae every tongue.

And honest toil, ye'll a' allow,
That is if Labour gets her due,
Lifts men aboon the idle crew
        Wha' seem to think
Nane but themsel's should e'er be fou
        O' meat or drink.

But aft on Misery's cauld bed
I grant that Toil must lay her head,
While underneath the sullen shade
        Of ill-got wealth,
The selfish indolent are laid
        To waste their health.

Yes! aften frae his humble cot,
The peasant on his hindmost groat,
Will see some pampered pensioned sot,
                    With haughty air,
Down pleasure's stream triumphant float,
                    Unscathed by care.

While he whose ill-rewarded toil
Compels the barren waste to smile,
Is doomed to see earth's fruits the spoil
                    Of that fell brood,
Who never deign a hand to soil
                    For mankind's good.

O! when will that blest time arrive,
When men some method will contrive
To banish from Industry's hive
                    The lazy drones,
Who long by fraud have learned to thrive
                    On Labour's groans.

Then future TENNANTS will arise,
Like those who raised me to the skies,
Some giant measure to devise –
                    That even steam,
With all its powers, will in men's eyes
                    A trifle seem.

Art has progressed, I say, but Time
Shall never see her in her prime,
For years will proudly in each clime
                    To years unfold
New wonders, that her course sublime
                    Will soon make old.

The lightening's vivid glances may,
Ere long, acknowledge mankind's sway,
And guide the swift bark on her way
                    Through seas unknown,
Where dreary Night 'mid icebergs grey
                    Has fixed her throne.

Yes! science shall the clouds dispel,
Beneath whose gloom sly birkies dwell,
Wha to their dupes some queer cracks tell
        About a chiel
Wha lang on earth has borne the bell –
        Ev'n Nick the deil.

But they ne'er try by demonstration,
Or algebraical equation,
To prove what no ane in this nation,
        Nor yet in France,
E'er saw, since first he led creation
        Sae rough a dance.

But I may let thae things alane,
Time will, himsel', or I'm mista'en,
See Mystery and a' her train
        To Reason yield,
And lay beneath Truth's sacred fane,
        Her broken shield.

Then War with her foul deeds no more
Will stain the earth with human gore,
Nor this be called a hostile shore,
        Because, perchance,
It lies o' miles perhaps a score
        Apart frae France.

Then Peace her olive branch will spread,
And a' its bland endearments shed
On those who – ne'er by folly led –
        Delight to stray,
Where Industry wi' lightsome tread,
        Has smoothed the way.

Then THOMSONS, McINTYRES, & Co.,
To wondering mortals yet will shew
Some piece of brickwork, that will throw
        Far in the shade
E'en me, who am, as ye all know,
        The best yet made.

But since they've gi'en me the comman'
(As PREMIER LUM) o'er a' the lan',
I promise you, hae there's my han',
   If I be spared,
To have a scheme weel planned an' drawn
    To get things squared.

Gie me *sax months* to glowr about,
An' faith I'll keep a sharp leuk out,
And watch how statesmen turn their snout
   To smell a job;
I'll no mak' sic a bungle o't
   As BRITHER BOB.

Now fare-ye-weel, I maun prepare
The labours o' the day to share,
And when we hae an hour to spare,
   We'll hae our joke;
Meantime, see how on upper air
   I spread my smoke.

John Mitchell, 1842

from Wee Charlie's Elegy

Poor Glasgow bodies noo may wail
Wi' ruefu' faces lang an' pale,
An' tears let fa' like patterin' hail,
   Or crystal bead,
While they tell o'er the waefu' tale,
   Wee Charlie's dead.

He was their leerie mony a year,
He kept their lampies burnin' clear,

'Mid stormy nichts, withouten fear,
       He onward sped,
But death has stopp'd his bright career –
       Wee Charlie's dead.

Ere he was made a leerie here,
He sailed the ocean far an' near,
An' fought the invader without fear,
       By Rodney led;
His country's weal was to him dear –
       Our hero's dead.

Folk said he had the second sicht,
An' he that didna do him richt,
He just cry'd *presto*, an' the wicht
       Lay cauld as lead,
But his *black airt* death couldna fricht,
       That laid him dead.

But, if he was a dark airt chiel',
He kent the licht airt just as weel,
For, be he saint or be he deil,
       His only trade
Was bringin' licht free dark, atweel –
       But Charlie's dead.

                   *

He ran alang the streets like spunkie,
An' speel'd the lather like a monkey,
Just like a wee conceited flunkie
       He cock'd his head,
But noo, alas! his wee short trunkie
       Lies cauld and dead.

Near fifty winters' win' an' weet
Ha'e blawn out o'er his auld grey pate,
Since he began to drive elate
       Wi' leerie's speed;
Aft wi' his torch he clear'd the gate –
       But noo he's dead.

                   *

Then ilka knight o' torch an' lather
Aroun' his bier in tears did gather,
An' mourn'd their auld respected brither,
             In blackest weed –
To match him noo there's scarce anither,
             Since Charlie's dead.

An' to St Mungo's auld kirk aisle
They bore him slow, in rank and file,
An' tears bedew'd their cheeks the while
             They lower'd his head.
The auldest leerie in the isle,
             Amen! is dead.

James Lemon, 1844

How We Spent a Sabbath Day

Our's is a wee dark unco crowded house,
Cramm'd in a strait an' foul owercrowded street;
We can afford nae better, an' whan loose
Frae six day's toil, I hameward turn my feet,
I'm glad at heart an' gratefu', as is meet,
For then God's hallow'd day comes roun' again;
Blest day of rest! the labour-weary see't,
An' rest on't through the six; it's made for men, –
A' gratitude to God that aye this day's our ain!

Ae Sabbath morn in June, God's sun his light
Shot in as free as our scrimp window let;
The scanty ray was but a grumly sight,
An' shewed the air we breath'd the fouler yet;
Yet purer far than our close mill is it,
Which made me thankfu' that our wife an' weans

104

Were even here, tho' wan aroun' me set, –
Tho' frail, yet free frae sicknesses an' pains,
An' fit tae worship God in gratefu' humble strains.

Our morning worship dune, I spak' tae May
To get hersel' an' a' the weans in trim,
For we abroad would keep this holy day;
She swithered, an' her e'e filled tae the trim; –
She read my motive! weel she kent how slim
An' lifeless were the weans, how feckless she,
How much a' needed change, – but doubts bedim;
She 'fear'd it wad be wrang; our elder, he
Had ca'd it awfu' sin tae spend the Sabbath sae.'

Dear May! I watched her fair complexion dwine,
I lang had seen her rosy colours fade,
An' day by day her cheerfu' bussle tine;
O what a change this dingy town has made,
Sin' first I brought her here my bonnie bride,
Frae faither's cottage, sheltered aff the blast
In woody loun upon the fresh hillside!
As for the weans, puir things! there ne'er did last
A bloom on infant's cheek whaur their young lot was cast.

She fain wad be persuaded, sae I read
How He wha spak as never man did speak,
Himsel' the truth, about His ain day said, –
'It's mercy and not sacrifice I seek.'
The great Preceptor He! hear Him ye meek,
Sin-fearing, toil-worn, city-pent-up poor:–
'Is't lawful to do good or ill, the weak
To kill or save, would ye your sheep endure
To fall into a pit nor lift it out secure?'

'But than a sheep much better is a man,
So 'ts lawful to do well on Sabbath day,'
He Godlike said, an' heal'd the withered han';
An' wherefore no our with'rin' health dear May
Seek tae revive, an eke our bairns' tae?
There's ne'er an hour that we by day can own

But this that God has gi'en us, should we stay; —
Min' that he teaches us tae understan'
That we may break his sixth, nor keep his fourth comman'.

An' can't we seek an' serve God onywhere, —
In kirk, at hame, in ony place or time?
He tell't her o' Samaria that not there,
Nor yet in hallowed auld Jerusalem,
Its holy hill or house, His ancient hame,
Would He be worship'd now, but in the heart
In spirit an' in truth; whaur in His name
Are twa or three met, there does He concert, —
There is He in the midst, His blessing to impart.

His word prevailed, the elder's lost its power;
Sae, a' things ready, see us on our road,
As seriously bent in that quiet hour
As e'er whan gaun tae kirk, tae honour God.
Twa weans were in our arms, twa bigger trod
Fu' happy at our fit, an' maybe yin
Ta'en frae us in the spring, frae's new abode
An angel now, was sent tae soar abune,
An' be our ministering spirit, though unseen!

A' ye wha drive your carriage or your cab,
An' work your man an' beast wi' but the view
Tae keep the Sabbath, liveried in drab,
Or humble hack, I fin' nae faut wi' you —
Nae doubt ye see't your duty sae tae do.
Ye'll fin nae faut that we took tae the rail?
We saw't wi' our young charge our duty too; —
Ye'll no, whatever prejudice prevail,
Cry sin on us, or puir folks' Sunday-coach assail?

But should ye, let this stop that cry o' yours: —
'Tak', hypocrite! your coach-pole out your e'e,
Then see tae pick the railway motes frae ours;'
An' tae a' ithers wha sae surely see
An' awfu' sin we've dune, we say that we
Are just as sure 'twas right, gratefu' we us'd

The railway – like God's ither creatures, free
Tae man an' guid, an' no tae be refused,
But ta'en wi' thankfu'ness an' no tae be abused.

We reached the station, quietly were set doun,
Quietly the train again passed on its way;
Nae fuss nor bussle ony whaur aroun'
Tae mar our errand on this blessed day.
We dauner'd slowly up a bonnie brae
An' sat us doun. – O what a rapture fill'd
Our souls, at sight o' summer's grand array!
But I'm toun born an' bred, an' little schuil'd,
Nor power hae tae describe the sight sic joy instilled.

How fragrant an' delicious was the air!
We drank o' health wi' every breath we drew;
An' needfu' was it tae my young anes there,
As tae the flower its morning meal the dew;
An' pleasant was the whiff the saft win' blew
Upon our keezened cheeks, an' sooght alang
Awa' ower lea an' hill; the bright sun threw
His sheen ower a', an' jouk'd the leaves amang,
Playin' merry wi' the burn which laugh'd, an' danc'd, an' sang!

A' sang God's praise in harmony; the breeze,
Profuse o' scented sweets, its safest tune
Play'd on its many-stringed harp, the trees;
They waving chim'd their several chords aroun',
The birds join'd sweetest notes o' various soun,
An' mellow dron'd its part the humming bee,
The mither ewe an' lamb their bleats sent doun,
The kye pour'd in their deep bass solemnly,
As did in mute heart harmony my wife an' me!

O what a growth o' soul got our first twa!
How did their minds expand! dear Tam an' Jean,
How much amaz'd wi' every thing they saw!
They glower'd aroun' wi' wonder-staring een,
An' speir'd sae greedily, an' drank sae keen
My answers in, ayont themselves wi' joy!

Nor e'er at kirk or Sabbath schuil, I ween,
  Gat weans sic langsome lessons, but did cloy,
However fit the task, or means ane might employ.

  Much tae be pitied are puir weans toun bred;
  They share the bit o' winter's frost an' snawin',
  But no for them are summer's wild flowers spread,
  Mine did nae ken a gowan when they saw ane;
  Nor heather, broom, nor whins, nor primrose blawin',
  That grow for weans; nor butterflee, nor bee,
  E'er saw before, nor heard the cuckoo ca'in';
  Nor wimplin' burn had seen, nor hill nor tree,
Till this soul-widenin' hour o' wond'rin extacy!

  Imagine now wi' what a tellin' power
  This lesson filled their souls – 'See God in a'!'
  I aft at hame had taught them this before,
  But ne'er they saw its force as noo they saw,
  An' felt, in their astonishment an' awe.
  An' tae this truth then gotten, wha shall say
  But that whan earth, an' sky, an' time's awa,
  Tae it, and tae our use made o' that day,
They'll own the joys an' glories o' eternity!

  Nor did we greater truths than thae forget, –
  The gospel mysteries o' our faith an' hope;
  Though a' ower young were Tam an' Jeannie yet
  Tae waud thae deeps, or wi' their wonders cope.
  An' noo the kirk hour's come, but May maun stop
  Frae that tae tent the weans, tae tak them there
  I ne'er could see't a guid, until the scope
  O that solemnity they ken o' mair,
An' something understan' o' sermon, praise, an' prayer.

  I join'd the worshippers, an' sat me doun:
  It matters na if they were *Bond*, or *Free*,
  Or *Freer*, – sweetly cam' the gospel soun'
  Frae the auld reverend minister tae me.
  An' unco difference was it here tae be
  In body, health refreshed, eident an' keen

108

A worshipper, frae whan I, earnest tae,
  In our town kirk in thowless health ha'e been
An' wearied 'gainst my will, as I ha'e aften seen.

  Atween the preachins by the burn we sat,
  Ahint a stately tree that screen'd the heat,
  An' ate our bit o' bread, an' drank o' that
  That ran sae cheaply by, – plain fare, but sweet,
  Kitchen'd wi' gratitude an appetite.
  An' noo the auld kirk bell cries 'come' again;
  An' May in turn gangs wi' the crowd that meet
  In house o' prayer, tae join in their amen,
Tae Him that heareth prayer, nor surely a' in vain!

  An' I was left the shepherd o' the flock;
  My youngest twa lay sleepin' on the green;
  An' ower the faither's soul deep feelin' broke,
  As my fond e'e bent ower them lang an keen. –
  For baith their souls' an' bodies' health, the scene
  Arous'd my great responsibility;
  An' aye since then my firm resolve has been
  Tae daur tae seek their weel as on that day,
An' thole thick-headed blame, an' brave loud bigotry!

  Belyve the kirk skail'd an' the thrang gaed by –
  Hale kintra folk, ne'er needin' health tae seek.
  Ae fresh auld man glower'd at us sour an' sly,
  An' dunch'd his frien', wha shuck his head sae sleek,
  Syne whisperin' passed, an' sidelins roun' did keek.
  Did they but think us desecrators? then,
  Ah! whaur was heaven-born charity, the meek,
  That thinks nae ill, believes an' hopes there's nane?
They judged as dae their betters, wha should better ken.

  The sun had passed the third stage on his road,
  As strong an' hale as he the day began;
  Sae true tae time, as fresh wi' a' its load,
  The hameward train intae the station ran;
  Quick aff we whirl'd, quick roun the world span!
  A wonderfu' creation is the rail!

I thought how great, how like tae God, is man,
An' ah how wee! a drink-made idiot, pale,
Sat by me maun'rin senseless oaths – alas, how frail!

'An' therefore stop the Sunday-trains,' they cry!
An' maun I sacrifice my wife an' weans, –
An' maun a' there for guid, for this, deny
Themsel's their due – for this, refuse the means
For benefit God's gi'en them, an' comply?
I've seen the like black scandal in God's house,
But wha for that sin sic a cure wad try,
An' lock kirk doors because o' sic misuse? –
God ne'er withdraws a privilege though some't abuse.

But every body there profan'd the day
They think, a maist uncharitable thought!
I canna read the heart, – some might dune sae;
But wha shall daur tae say I sinn'd in ought
O' my intentions, seekin' what I sought?
An' mony there might haen as guid intent;
Daur I say no – shall ithers, kennin' nought?
Yet serious thought, if some the day mis-spent!
But sae it sometimes is, even in the kirk, profan't.

While thus I chew'd the cud we reach'd the town:
Sae few the minutes ta'en, I'm free tae say
Our twa trips out an' in were quicker dune
Than langsyne journey o' a Sabbath day –
A priv'lege fourth-commaun bound-Jews had aye.
Arriv'd at hame, the wife an' I the day's
Jaunt cracket ower, improvin't by the way;
An' at its close, our hearts an' voices raise
Wi' gratitude an' thankfu'ness, in prayer an' praise.

An' thus we spent a happy Sabbath day!
Was't rightly spent? if sae, how mony mair
Are there that need the like, how mony tae
Wad use the priv'lege weel wi' holy care.
O that a' parties would arrange th' affair,
As that ae train were run – for puir wark folk

A corner o't sae cheap, that they could spare
    Tae pay for't; an' should some mak' this a cloak
For sin, the same at hame would have the Sabbath broke.

    'I would not like to have the health thus got
    By Sabbath desecration,' – this ance said
    Our minister; – May God forgi'e an' blot
    The awsome statement out he preachin' made.
    He's a weel meanin' man, an' thus I pray'd;
    For like the fou man in the train, I wot
    He kent na what he spak'. I'll no upbraid; –
    He needed na, may it ne'er be his lot
Tae need God's day tae seek what me and mine had sought.

    A word anent the men that work the train. –
    I ken o' wark, an' like my Sunday rest
    Ower weel, tae wish it ta'en frae toil-worn men;
    But o' twa ills, tae choose the less is best; –
    If by the wark o' twa-three hours at maist,
    By twa-three men in turn, each Sabbath day,
    A train were run – it's but a sma' request,
    Whan aff sae mony 'twould be seldom tae,
But the amount o' guid tae hunders wha can say!

    I dinna enter in tae ither cases
    O Sabbath mercy an' necessity,
    Tho' doubtless sic a pop'lous toun as this is
    Has mony, mony ev'ry Sabbath day
    That maun be dune; a train wad help for thae,
    An' desecration save in wark an' time.
    O that Christ's rule – 'Even as ye would tak', gie',
    Alliance Christians would but mak' their aim!
How would they like it tried tae shut their kirks frae them?

    But say a kind o' consciencious men –
    'We grant this view is scriptural an' right,
    But if allow'd, we dread it might exten';
    A' kinds o' wark wad follow, till there might
    Be nought o' sabbath left.' Nae second sight
    Ha'e we; ne'er fear tae trust God's day tae's care;

Opening of the Glasgow and Garnkirk Railway, 1831 (D. O. Hill) MITCHELL LIBRARY

Whate'er befa', let's act up tae our light.
Fearin' results does duty aft deter;
We're prone tae judge, an' speak, an' act for God – an' err.

Anonymous, *c.*1846

Clyde Street, *c.*1850 (Robert Carrick) MITCHELL
LIBRARY

The Street

Flow on, dark Street! I hear thee roar
   Throughout the noisy noon,
Louder than billows on the shore,
   Beneath the muffled moon.
Flow on! each dusky human wave
Shall yet find silence in the grave.

Flow on! what faces line thy sides!
   What looks of care and crime
Swell out those hourly ebbing tides
   That fill the gaps of time.
At midnight, spectral sorrow stalks
Adown thy dark deserted walks.

To thee a solace Darkness lends –
   She stills thy weary wars;
And Midnight, like a mother, bends
   Her beating heart of stars,
O'er souls that sin, o'er eyes that weep,
O'er children smiling in their sleep.

Oft through thy silent mesh of homes
   A tingling terror flies,
The lightning-winged alarum comes
   In fire athwart the skies,
When, with a gush of smoky light
A conflagration scares the night.

The engines thunder down thee, Street,
   Sleep startles with a scream,
To hear the onward flood of feet,
   And with that ghastly gleam,
We see, through curtains wildly drawn,
The midnight like a dismal dawn.

Dark Street! I know thine inmost heart,
 In thee my years were nurst;
O could thy donjon lips dispart!
 O could thy cold heart burst!
What aching tales to earth were given –
Stern secrets held by thee and heaven!

And creeping oft, like some dark thought,
 Across thy dream of gain,
From Sorrow's wailing chamber brought,
 Flows on a funeral train:
Grim jest upon this fleeting breath!
Pass – painful pageantry of death!

Oft have I watched thy windows blaze,
 Like pools of liquid gold,
When, in a shroud of fiery haze,
 The dying sun was rolled,
And, from the golden-gated west,
Dun evening bared her burning breast.

Flow, Fashion, through thy channel flow!
 Roar, Commerce, down thy stream!
Roar on! a thousand years ago
 Thy being was a dream:
Another thousand, it may be –
But no, we dare not think of thee.

James Macfarlan, 1855

A Tale of the Town

'Mong sunny plains or waving woods,
   Alas! I was not born;
I never heard in solitudes
   The music of the morn;
I never nursed a poet's dream
Where raindrops dance upon the stream.

My home o'erhung a narrow lane
   Where woe and want were paired,
Where vice o'erflowing ebb'd again,
   And stealthy crime was laired;
And from my window stretched for miles
A dreary wilderness of tiles.

As some poor bird, within its wires,
   Knows when the spring is nigh,
And to the heaven of song aspires;
   So, in the city, I,
Immured amid the toiling throng,
Consoled my captive heart with song.

My walks were not upon the plains,
   Nor 'mong dew-heavy leaves,
But where amid the streets and lanes
   The heart of tumult heaves;
And where the night-black river glides,
The sepulchre of suicides.

My sights were not the setting sun,
   Sowing with gold the sea,
But some new phase of vice begun –
   Some end of misery;
Or when through fog the red sun broke,
Seen faintly as a fire through smoke.

And oft at night I stood beside
  The glooming range of ships,
When to the quays rose high the tide
  And laved their granite lips,
And saw the moon, as if through bars,
Check'd by the vessels' masts and spars.

I lived in hope that some bright hour
  Would spring from barren years,
A sunbeam on my path – a flower
  Long water'd by my tears.
At last there came a holiday,
Wild as a bird I dashed away.

Oh, when I felt each weary limb
  Among the cooling grass,
And watched, until my sight grew dim,
  The fair cloud phantoms pass,
Methought that it were sweet to die
Beneath the clear and open sky.

Again upon my senses beat
  The city's wave-like din,
And, as in furrows, in each street
  Are sown the seeds of sin.
I'm in the streets: but *that* bright day
Has kept my heart in fields away!

James Macfarlan, 1855

from The Wanderer

Mighty furnaces are flaring like a demon's breath of fire,
Forges, like great burning cities, break in many a crimson spire;
Tongues of eager flame are lapping all the glory of the heaven,
While a blush of burning hectic o'er the midnight's face is driven.
Peals the thunder throat of labour, hark! the deaf'ning anvils clash,
Like a thousand angry sabres in a battle's headlong dash.
Hear the thoroughfares of tumult, like the midnight ocean's roar
As in agony he clutches at the black heart of the shore.
Toiling there the poor boy-poet, grimed, within a dismal den,
Piles the fire, and wields the hammer, jostled on by savage men;
Burns his life to mournful ashes on a thankless hearth of gloom,
For a paltry pittance digging life from out an early tomb.
And the soul is dwarfed within him that was cast in Titan mould,
And the wealth of heaven he loses for the lack of human gold,
And he cannot see the stars arise in splendid sheen of light,
Like angel watchfires gleaming on the cloudy cliffs of night!

James Macfarlan, 1857

Glasgow

Sing, Poet, 'tis a merry world;
That cottage smoke is rolled and curled
   In sport, that every moss
Is happy, every inch of soil; –
Before *me* runs a road of toil
   With my grave cut across.
Sing, trailing showers and breezy downs –
I know the tragic heart of towns.

City! I am true son of thine;
Ne'er dwelt I where great mornings shine
   Around the bleating pens;
Ne'er by the rivulets I strayed,
And ne'er upon my childhood weighed
   The silence of the glens.
Instead of shores where ocean beats,
I hear the ebb and flow of streets.

Black Labour draws his weary waves,
Into their secret-moaning caves;
   But with the morning light,
That sea again will overflow
With a long weary sound of woe,
   Again to faint in night.
Wave am I in that sea of woes,
Which, night and morning, ebbs and flows.

I dwelt within a gloomy court,
Wherein did never sunbeam sport;
   Yet there my heart was stirr'd –
My very blood did dance and thrill,
When on my narrow window-sill,
   Spring lighted like a bird.
Poor flowers – I watched them pine for weeks,
With leaves as pale as human cheeks.

Afar, one summer, I was borne;
Through golden vapours of the morn,
   I heard the hills of sheep:
I trod with a wild ecstasy
The bright fringe of the living sea:
   And on a ruined keep
I sat, and watched an endless plain
Blacken beneath the gloom of rain.

O fair the lightly sprinkled waste,
O'er which a laughing shower has raced!
   O fair the April shoots!
O fair the woods on summer days,

Some kindred with my human heart
    Lives in thy streets of stone;
For we have been familiar more
Than galley-slave and weary oar.

The beech is dipped in wine; the shower
Is burnished; on the swinging flower
    The latest bee doth sit.
The low sun stares through dust of gold,
And o'er the darkening heath and wold
    The large ghost-moth doth flit.
In every orchard Autumn stands,
With apples in his golden hands.

But all these sights and sounds are strange;
Then wherefore from thee should I range?
    Thou hast my kith and kin;
My childhood, youth, and manhood brave;
Thou hast that unforgotten grave
    Within thy central din.
A sacredness of love and death
Dwells in thy noise and smoky breath.

Alexander Smith, 1857

The Broomielaw, c.1860 (William Graham) MITCHELL LIBRARY

from A Boy's Poem

The morn rose blue and glorious o'er the world;
The steamer left the black and oozy wharves,
And floated down between dark ranks of masts.
We heard the swarming streets, the noisy mills;
Saw sooty foundries full of glare and gloom,
Great bellied chimneys tipped by tongues of flame,
Quiver in smoky heat. We slowly passed
Loud building-yards, where every slip contained
A mighty vessel with a hundred men
Battering its iron sides. A cheer! a ship
In a gay flutter of innumerous flags
Slid gaily to her home. At length the stream
Broadened 'tween banks of daisies, and afar

The shadows flew upon the sunny hills;
And down the river, 'gainst the pale blue sky,
A town sat in its smoke. Look backward now!
Distance has stilled three hundred thousand hearts,
Drowned the loud roar of commerce, changed the proud
Metropolis which turns all things to gold,
To a thick vapour o'er which stands a staff
With smoky pennon streaming on the air.

Alexander Smith, 1857

The Gallant Shoemakers of Glasgow

Air – *The Roving Journeyman*

Come all ye gallant shoemakers wherever you may be,
I pray you give attention and listen unto me;
In the year of fifty-seven, boys, when spring-time it came round,
We vowed to raise our wages in famous Glasgow town.

A meeting then was called in the Minerva Hall,
And speakers there explained to us our wages were too small;
But we would have them up again our happiness to crown,
And prove ourselves bold journeymen in famous Glasgow town.

A vote it then was taken, likewise a show of hands,
All by our loyal chairman, who waited our commands;
The committee did smile in glee, and master's men did frown,
For all the men were ready there in famous Glasgow town.

Oh! if that our employers had only heard the cheers,
It would have broke their hearts, my boys, and caus'd them to shed tears,
To think that we would all unite whom they thought to keep down,
But the journeymen are all true flints in famous Glasgow town.

So ye gallant crafts be steady in both the east and west,
And likewise the Cowcaddens, which has been long opprest;
Stand fast like loyal Britons and the day shall be your own –
Bold Irish hearts act well your parts in famous Glasgow town.

And what though we should tramp, my boys, we've often tramp'd before,
Before that we would 'scab' it, lads, we'll tramp the country o'er;
Our lasses fair will welcome us, and never on us frown,
For they love the gallant journeymen of famous Glasgow town.

So success to ev'ry journeyman that ever pull'd a hair,
And success to ev'ry journeyman that ever shopp'd a pair;
Success to Judge and Donaldson who fear no master's frown,
And success to all the gallant flints of famous Glasgow town.

Anonymous, 1857

Glasgow Fair

Air – *Maggie Lauder*

Oh, never gang to Glasgow Fair,
   Amang the scolding lasses,
For hundreds of them's gathered there,
   An' 'mang them there's a' classes.
Oh, kintra lads tak' my advice,
   And never, you, gang near them,
Nae decent lads wad speir their price,
   Nae decent men could bear them.

I saw the fule come on the stage,
   Price of admission crying,
The audience een he did engage,
   Folk to the shows cam' flying.

The clown stands beating at his drum,
    And a' their instruments glancing,
The bagpipes yell and organs bum,
    And show loons tight-rope dancing.

A strumpet she comes up to me
    And asks me for a mutchkin,
Na, na, quo' I, I ken na thee,
    Quo' she, I'm Miss McCutchen.
Weel I kent your sister Kate,
    Langsyne we lived thegither,
And mony a nicht we've been out late,
    Toozlin' wi' ane anither.

Into a tavern us twa gaed,
    Syne ca'd for half-a-mutchkin,
And a' the expenses I defrayed,
    To treat this Miss McCutchen.
Quo' she to me, that's gae and guid,
    Oh let me hae some mair o't;
Quo' I to her, ye drucken jade,
    Ye're unco ill to sair o't.

She at my person sly did keek,
    The time the glass she licked,
And when I drapped owre asleep,
    She baith my pouches picked.
Noo kintra lads ye've heard my tale,
    Ne'er deal in half-mutchkins,
And when you come near Glasgow Jail
    Watch you the Miss McCutchens.

William Burns, 1857

Heaven Knows

Lines on the Trial of Madeleine Smith for the Murder of L'Angelier

Shade of the hapless stranger, lost L'Angelier,
   Whose life's young light was quenched in guilt and shame,
Say, haunt'st thou still the lane, the fatal gate,
   Where to thy arms the fair, false syren came?

We seek not now thy 'merits to disclose,
   Or draw thy frailties from their dread abode';
We would not sit in judgment on the man
   Whose soul hath stood before the bar of God.

'Not proven' was thy thrice-repeated deed,
   Thou of the stony heart and dauntless eye:
Smile not; in Heaven's high court thou yet shalt hear
   The unerring proven verdict of the sky.

A lovely isle lies cradled in the deep,
   Its flowery glades embowered in fruitful trees,
A weeping mother wanders on the beach
   And pours her sorrows on the seaward breeze.

Ah! to her widowed heart her only son
   She last had clasped upon that island shore;
He came, he saw, he loved, he sinned, he died –
   We wait till Heaven and time shall tell us more.

Janet Hamilton, 1857

Madeleine Hamilton Smith, 1835–1928 (John Urie, 1856)
MITCHELL LIBRARY

Lightburn Glen

Air – *There was a Lass, and she was fair*

There is a spot I dearly lo'ed,
   When I was summers nine or ten,
Where slender blue-bells wav'd and woo'd
   Young barefoot wanderers to that glen.
So shy the wagtail bobb'd and bow'd –
   A mystery was the little wren –
And purple berries there were pu'd
   By laughin' bands in Lightburn Glen.

When gloamin breath'd upon thy stream,
   And hush'd the song of roaming bee,
Ere yet the moon had lent her beam
   To make thee lovelier, if might be;
Then still the lark proclaimed thy praise,
   And challeng'd in his song divine
Those glorious two, whose mellow lays
   Charm'd the dark woods of Carntyne.

Another beauty met my gaze
   In riper years, with all to join –
That lark might ne'er attempt to praise,
   Nor all the choir of Carntyne.
If ye ha'e woo'd and hae'na won,
   By dewy loan or leafy den;
There's no a place below the sun
   I'd sooner try than Lightburn Glen.

William Miller, 1863

Let Glasgow Flourish

I   THE MONKISH PERIOD

LONG, long ago, when monkish zeal
Controll'd all for the common weal;
When kirks were built, and mass was sung,
When men were gagg'd, both old and young.

Ere freemen spoke what freemen felt,
When all beneath the mitre knelt –
When blazon'd banners flaunted free,
And rhymes explained dark heraldry.

Thus: – Here's the bell that never rang,
And here's the fish that never swam,
Here's to the bird that never flew,
From off the tree that never grew.
      Hurrah! Let Glasgow Flourish.

II   THE MARTIAL PERIOD

Long, long ago, the monks are dead,
And soldier craft sprung up instead;
Still men were chain'd in thought and word,
And justice wore a bloody sword.

Then honour cut a throat for gold,
And tales of strife were glibly told.
Even then, the selfish monkish rhyme
Was sung to consecrate a crime.

Fight for the bell that never rang,
Strike for the fish that never swam,
Raise high the bird that never flew,
Stand for the tree which never grew.
      Hurrah! Let Glasgow Flourish!

Glasgow Cathedral, *c*.1782 (Thomas Hearne)

Panoramic view of Glasgow, *c*.1835 (James Anderson)

Cathcart Bridge, 1842 (William Simpson)

Govan on the Clyde, 1842 (William Simpson)

Gorbals steeple, 1845 (William Simpson)

Todd and Higginbottam's Mill from Glasgow Green, winter morning, *c.*1847
(William Simpson)

Saltmarket, 1849 (Alexander Shanks)

Trongate, 1849 (William Simpson)

Port Dundas, *c.*1850 (William Simpson)

Glasgow Cross, *c.*1850 (William Simpson)

Trongate, *c.*1850 (Alexander Shanks)

Two Kids Scribbling on a Wall by Joan
Eardley, *c.*1955 (George Oliver)

Finnieston Crane (Valerie Thornton)

Clydegrad (Edwin Morgan)

Roystonhill (Valerie Thornton)

Glasgow Green Carnival (Edwin Morgan)

III   THE MERCANTILE PERIOD

Long, long ago, both cowl and sword,
Which slaves obey'd and fools ador'd,
Are dust; now merchants fill the land,
And truth and honour, hand in hand

Walk through the streets; no huxtering guile
Entraps you with a heartless smile;
All fraud is fled, but still the rhyme
Lives green, and mocks at gnarl'd time.

Buy now the tree that never grew,
Barter the bird that never flew,
Sell all the fish that never swam,
Coin down the bell that never rang.
         Hurrah! Let Glasgow Flourish!

IV   THE MENDICANT PERIOD

No sneering cynic now can tell
Of thumb-breadth robb'd from every ell,
Or griping bargains with the poor;
No weavers beg from door to door.

No raggedness e'er meets the eye,
No starv'd poor die in agony;
Then mourn not for the olden time,
When people sang the monkish rhyme.

But rob the tree that never grew,
Pluck clean the bird that never flew,
Skin, gut, the fish that never swam,
And pledge the bell that never rang.
         Hurrah! Let Glasgow Flourish.

V   THE MERCENARY PERIOD

Respice finem. Leech attend,
Credit is sick. Say will it mend?

No longer fear we flimsy bills,
Or flashy shops and empty tills.

Cash is not lavish'd on the church,
Nor creditors left in the lurch;
The bankrupt pays his trusting friend,
With nought per cent of dividend.

Tricks never bolster rotten trade,
No fortunes squander'd e'er they're made;
Then sigh not for the ancient time,
But sing this true and modern rhyme.

The tree, a bank with cash all gone,
The bird, a merchant credit blown,
The fish, a victim shrunk and bare,
The bell, the clang of wild despair.
                Hurrah! Let Glasgow Flourish.

VI   THE MILLENNIAL PERIOD

A glorious scene looms dim but far,
Where men have lost the art of war;
There poor men are not bought and sold,
And truth out-weighs the miser's gold.

There virtue is a priceless thing,
With higher rank than lord or king;
There love and joy, of heavenly birth,
Have banish'd falsehood from the earth.

There faith in man and faith in God,
Make smooth the traveller's upward road;
There hope's bright beacon lights the way,
Fore-shadowing man's true destiny.

There charity in word and deed,
Knits all mankind, of every creed,
Then from the reason-waken'd world,
Are bigotry and priest-craft hurl'd.

Men mourn not then the ancient time,
But thus translate the monkish rhyme: –
Man's life, a green and spreading tree,
With fruitage for eternity.

His mind, like bird in ambient air,
Soars through a boundless atmosphere,
And like the fish with mystic ring,
Vast stores of knowledge loves to bring

From fire, from earth, from air, from sea,
Uncheck'd save by infinity.
Then wind-borne, hark! The passing bell
Rings vice and ignorance's knell.

Such is the hallow'd age of gold,
By Christ the son of man foretold;
When man shall trust his brother's word,
And God alone shall be adored.
            Till then, Let Glasgow Flourish!

James Manson, 1863

from A Welcome to the Waters of Loch-Katrine

Thou comest to a city where men untimely die,
Where hearts in grief are swelling, and cheeks are seldom dry –
A city where merchant princes to Mammon basely kneel,
While those that drag the idol's car are crushed beneath the wheel.

Throughout her mighty system of tunnel and tube and main,
Thy healthful current is pulsing, pulsing through every vein;

THE FAMILY DINNER.

The Family Dinner, 1886 (W. Mitchell, *Rescue the Children*)
MITCHELL LIBRARY

In the fever den, in the attic, in cellars under the street,
The poor have long been waiting to quaff thy waters sweet.

Thou comest in thy beauty, like Godiva, long ago,
To save our sin-curst city from a tax of death and woe –
To cool the fire of the fever, and quench the fever of lust –
To moisten the lips of the dying, and moisten the poor man's crust.

O that from his inner vision thou could'st wash the scales of sin,
That thro' the darkened window heaven's glory might come in;
Restore to the cheeks of childhood the roses shed too soon,
And their infant lips will bless thee, for health is a precious boon!

O quench the fiery spirit that maddens the workman's brain,
That drags down reason from her throne, and riots in every vein,
Ere the stream becomes a river, and the river an ocean broad,
A dreary separating gulf betwixt his soul and God!

O would thy gushing waters might quench for ever and aye
Those fountains of fiery ruin that lead men's souls astray;
That drunkeries all were abolished, and, planted in their stead,
The reading-room and the school-room, and shops for the sale of bread!

James Nicholson, 1863

from My New Location

The whauraboots o' this location
Graced wi' the bardie's habitation,
Is brawly kent to Glasca bodies,
Coal-drawin' naigs, and weary cuddies.
It stauns hard-by the darksome runnel,
Kent as 'the Caledonian tunnel',
Through whilk, wi' bodies, gear, and cattle,
Fiz-fizen locomotives rattle,
Lang after Phœbus, glowin' fallow,
Has owre the wastlan hills shot hallow
'Mid ocean tides to cool and wallow.
In hurry-burry, yet in order,
Big trains frae baith sides o' the border –
'Tween Norlan', Thurso, and Slamannan,
'Tween auld Carlisle and busy Lunnan –
Or gaun or comin' still are birlin',
Wi' deavsome dunnerin' and dirlin',
The while the whistlin' and the skirlin'
Frae oot the roadster's steamy gullet
Rings through ane's lug-drum like a bullet.
Sic sichts an' soun's as my auld grannie,
Were she but here, wad thocht uncannie;
And as for railway-coach, to sit in't,
The ne'er o' her wad put a fit in't,
But wi' a gratefu' 'Gude be thankit',
Her ilka gate she'd blythely shank it.

As lordly ha's wi' groves and parks
Are bounded, sae wi' public warks
In busy, smeeky combination,
Is thickly hedged my new location.
My front has Tennant's muckle stauk,
Its brither, Townsend's, at my back;
Coalhills abune, and lower boundaries

Are potteries, secret warks, and found'ries,
Glass warks, distilleries, and smiddies,
Sichts, soun's, and smells, and a' that guid is.

There's rowth o' steer and botheration
Enow aboot my new location,
Though an' a month or twa were roun'
I dootna things 'ill settle doun:
A street side o' new houses biggin,
There's masons hewin', navvies diggin';
And muckle din there is and clamour
'Tween wooden mallet, axe, and hammer.
While to ane's door there's nae approachin',
For joists and quarry stanes encroachin'
Till, haith, at gaun I'm sic a bummel,
I'm fleyt some day I'll get a tumble,
And break a leg, or kilt be fairly,
Syne Meg, puir thing, wad miss me sairly.

As for the men 'bout my location,
Puir chiels, they're o' the toilin' station:
There's masons, plumbers, joiners, sawers;
There's moulders, potters, bottle-blawers;
Wi' railway guards, and engine ca'ers,
Coal-riddlers, carters, bakers, millers;
Mechanics, smiths, asphalte-distillers,
And twarie burly whisky sellers –
Thae lazy drones, whase avocation
Begets sic scenes o' desolation,
As ane sees plainly when he passes
The hive-hames o' the toilin' masses.
O whan will Common Sense see cause
(Excuse a parenthetic clause)
To stop this everlasting drain
Upon Industry's dearest vein?
Whan banish to its native hell
The vampire demon o' the stell?

O' wives and weans, but rarely scanty
'Mang workin' folk, they're here in plenty.

The weans, puir things, like feck o' ithers,
Bear strong resemblance to their mithers:
Some fat, some lean, some scant o' cleedin',
Some clad, weel-train'd, some scant o' breedin'!
Some cleanly-keepit, tosh an' cosie,
Some i' the gutters lank an' lousy,
Some cuddlin' i' their mithers' bosie.
Some mithers here grace wedded lives,
Some mithers are, yet arena wives;
Some decent, thrifty wives that wud be,
Ithers nae better than they should be –
Tho' sic are rife, an' mair's the pity,
In kintra village, toun, an' city.
Some plainly dress'd, some gaudy queans,
Wha glory in their crinolines;
Some real carefu', sober wives,
Some blasters o' their partners' lives,
Or at their door-cheeks idle stanin',
Or wi' their cronies boozin', pawnin'.

John Young, 1864

Dedicated to the People of Glasgow

Let Glasgow flourish, not in wealth alone,
But more in that which can so well atone
For want of gold – the lasting wealth of truth,
Which feeds that life that blooms in endless youth.
Let Clyde hold on, and still victorious be,
To plant her first-class ships on every sea.
Along her banks let commerce heap its piles,
And docks extend in long and tedious miles.
May hammer-clang from forge and workshop ring,
And honest toil its due reward still bring.

Let wealth flow in at energy's command,
And plenty spread her board on every hand.
Thus, like the blood that flows in healthy veins,
Alike dispersed and free from giddy pains.
May laws and habits give our honest toil,
To take their share, and hold their rightful spoil.
Not slaves in youth, and paupers in old age,
Begrimed with grief, and dying in a rage;
But skilled to work, and wise to use their means
Increasing funds, each year above their teens.

Let Glasgow flourish, with her clattering mills,
Dispersing wealth like fertilizing rills.
And may those streams of sprightly toiling youth,
Be free from vice and stamped with living truth.
May they be found in life's most hopeful grade,
The nation's wealth in higher sense than trade.
On these, O Scotland, keep a parent's eye,
Nor think that they were made in slums to die.
Leave them a prey to grasping, heartless greed,
That builds dark holes, where it and death may feed
On care-spent flesh, and infants weak in life,
That gasp and die in foul, unequal strife!
If thus you act, then, Scotland, strip thy crown,
And, self-debased, in contempt cast it down,
A retrograde in culture's noble race;
Go hug thy gold, and live in vile disgrace.
Oh! for that patriot's heart that once was yours,
That willed and worked, till dark benighted moors
Waved with a crop, whose cheering, gladsome fame,
Stamped on thy brow, a rare, a noble name.
Not gold, as now, the germ of active life,
But sense of duty nerved her arm for strife.
She viewed each soul that breathed her bracing air,
As cast by God upon her conscious care;
And grasping fast the means at her command,
A teeming crop appeared throughout her land.

Let Glasgow strive, till on her streets be seen
A virtuous race, from drunken vice made clean.

Feel that each soul is in itself a world,
For light prepared, or else to darkness hurled.
Why force your drunken traps upon the poor,
As poachers plant their gins upon a moor?
You first prepare them in the sickly slum,
For cheering draughts of whisky, gin, and rum.
Deprived of air, of light, and open space,
Effects are easy from such cause to trace:
The spirits sink, and self-respect goes down;
The ruling thought is how one best may drown
Incessant achings which are felt within,
And whisper peace through spirits, rum and gin.
Then sallying forth to open space and air,
Where'er they look, a public-house is there.
At every corner, passage, close, and gap,
No egress left without a spirit trap.
That none may pass without being tempted to err,
Upon the poor man's grocer you confer
A right to tempt his children and his wife,
Where they must go to buy the staff of life.
Pause, Scotland, pause! your bleeding wound review,
Rise to your time, to what you were prove true;
Upon the threshold of your sacred morn,
What drunken vomit that a beast might scorn!

Let Glasgow flourish in remodelled homes,
Not heaped and piled like cells in honey-combs.
Your fields are broad and free on every side,
Why jam your dwellings like a pent-up tide?
Why still adhere to antiquated plans,
And stack your houses in unsightly lands?
Shall steam in vain extend its potent hand,
And point the road to boundless tracts of land?
Is want of air, of light, and open space,
To go for nothing in our golden race?
Can human beings herd like flocks of sheep,
And yet their health and morals safely keep?
The narrow close, the long, clandestine stair,
Present to youth a dangerous moral snare.
The good, the bad, the virtuous, and corrupt,

Meet in the close, and climb the stair abrupt.
And then for health it cannot answer well –
It's still a draft, or else a stagnant well.

O Glasgow, keep thy country's sacred trust –
Not gold that flies as fast as vernal dust,
Which cannot bless you while it fills the heart,
But only plays deception's subtle part.
The Sabbath you to God his portion pledge;
Why trade to twelve, and steal it o'er the hedge?
Then half-refreshed, you struggle from your bed,
Not God to praise, but sleep the preacher dead.
Six days cannot suffice to buy and sell,
But at their close the people rush pell-mell,
As if in prison all the previous week,
And had no time, what each might need to seek.

Let Glasgow be a light upon a hill,
To commerce, trade, and persevering skill;
Still more a light in learning, truth, and grace,
That with the first, she still may take her place.
Her schools and college bless her toiling mass,
For as it should, they never served a class.
Like heaven's light, they took a nobler aim,
Here class is lost – to all the fount's the same.
While peer and peasant meet their lamps to light,
Distinctions vanish like the clouds of night.
Here studious worth from every class can rise,
For all alike may enter for the prize.
With growing lustre may they ever shine,
And shed reflected light in every clime.

Richard Pearson, 1865

Address to the Factory of Messrs J. & W. I. Scott & Co, John Street, Bridgeton

Hail! Royal Sovereign of the Factory race,
    Thrice do I hail thee on thy gorgeous throne;
And in thy queen-like lineaments I trace
    Thy worth as matchless as it is unknown.
How vast are thy dominions and thy wealth?
Thou hold'st a city's commerce by thyself.

The faithful porter at thy monarch gate,
    Through thy long arch doth cast his watchful eyes,
No stragglers see thee in thy queen-like state,
    Nor see thy royal structures round thee rise;
Nor enter thy back shed, so large and grand,
The boast of Scotland's manufacturing land.

Thy cotton palace from my left doth stand,
    A gem that England's cotton lords might prize;
Thy counting-house is placed at my right hand,
    Where will ye find its match, 'tis such a size?
And o'er thy snowy walls of massive pile
The king of commerce seems to sit and smile.

And when I cross thy wide expanding court,
    Hundreds of thy daughters I meet there;
Their young eyes lighted up with gladsome sport,
    Their handsome forms and faces, sweet and fair.
O! lovely Sovereign! thou dost bear the fame
Of daughters fair that wear a fairer name.

Thy sons, too, are the bravest of the brave,
    Their fame is spread throughout the Scottish land;
Love, truth, and honour, o'er their head doth wave,

And duty sways them both in heart and hand:
And thy cross-over-looms can truly tell,
Few with their skilful genius can excel.

Give to thy stockers every honour due,
    Thy pickers, carders, spinners, act their part;
Thy engineers, and thy mechanics, too,
    Are all sufficient in mechanic art.
Thy tapers, twisters, tenters, well may boast
Of many honours other men have lost.

Thy clerks, too, are a class of active men,
    So civil and polite in every form;
With unassuming grace they use their pen,
    Their faces free from cold contemptuous scorn,
And all thy managers, they are the same –
True to their trust – what more could duty claim?

But listen yet, I have a tale to tell,
    It is of younger years, when life was sweet,
Long ere you came into this land to dwell,
    I lived a happy child in Muslin Street;
And where thou standest now, I've gathered flowers,
And spent my sweetest, purest – childhood hours.

Near Edward's church, there stood an old grey wall,
    And further on a long green avenue –
O'er one side, many a clustering branch did fall,
    And on the other, a lovely hawthorn grew;
Oh! God, could memory die, and hide from sight
Those early scenes that haunt me day and night.

Old Father Time hath changed the scenes since then,
    And who shall call the tale I tell untrue;
Thy gorgeous arch that now inspires my pen,
    Stands on the spot where stood that avenue,
And where I sat in childhood's sunny smile,
I stand each day now at my daily toil.

And I am also changed – Fate's hand hath passed,
    And branded dark misfortunes on my brow;
O'er my young heart she breathed her withering blast.
    And like the leaves that fall from autumn's bough,
She scattered my young hopes unto the wind,
And left me here a leafless stem behind.

But, like a child, I'll cling unto thy breast,
    For there the milk of human kindness flows;
And whilst thou wear the crown – 'tis my request,
    That thou thy philanthropic love will show,
And let me ever kneel before thy shrine,
Rejoicing still – prosperity is thine.

Ellen Johnston, 1867

Wanted in Glasgow

Wanted a filter, to filter the Clyde,
    After some hundreds of people have died,
Chancing to fall in its poisonous tide;
Those who fall in there are likely to bide,
And if they have opened their mouths very wide
    They may as well stay, for when dragged out and dried
    'Twill be found that although they're not drowned they have died
Merely by trying the taste of the Clyde.
Wanted a corner in which one may hide
Away from the smoke that is spread far and wide;
From the factory chimneys on every side,
    By which folks in Glasgow like herrings are dried.
    To cure the smoke nuisance has nobody tried,
Of all the good folks that in Glasgow abide?
    'No smoking allowed!' might be here well applied.
Wanted a little more national pride

To sort this great city on every side;
To sweep up the streets and the rubbish to hide.
Wanted more street cars. It's awful to ride
Jammed down the middle and crammed down each side,
  'Twouldn't be very much worse to be fried!
  Wanted to know when some means will be tried
  By which all those wants can be quickly supplied,
That Glasgow may flourish, her citizens' pride.

Marion Bernstein, 1876

A Song of Glasgow Town

I'll sing a song of Glasgow town,
That stands on either side
The river that was once so fair,
The much insulted Clyde.
That stream, once pure, but now so foul,
Was never made to be
A sewer, just to bear away
The refuse to the sea.
Oh, when will Glasgow's factories
Cease to pollute its tide,
And let the Glasgow people see
The beauty of the Clyde!

I'll sing a song of Glasgow town:
On every side I see
A crowd of giant chimney stalks
As grim as grim can be.
There's always smoke from some of them –
Some black, some brown, some grey.
Yet genius has invented means
To burn the smoke away.
Oh, when will Glasgow factories

Cease to pollute the air;
To spread dull clouds o'er sunny skies
That should be bright and fair!

I'll sing a song of Glasgow town,
Where wealth and want abound;
Where the high seat of learning dwells
Mid ignorance profound.
Oh, when will Glasgow make a rule
To do just what she ought –
Let starving bairns in every school
Be fed as well as taught!
And when will Glasgow city be
Fair Caledonia's pride,
And boast her clear unclouded skies,
And crystal-flowing Clyde?

Marion Bernstein, 1876

First Fittin'

It's time that some sensible body should speak,
    For what in the world gars women and men
Gang scamperin' mad ower an auld-fashioned freak,
    That gangs by the name o' 'first fittin'', ye ken.

They will stan' for an 'oor in the snaw and the rain,
    When the year in the deed-thraws is wearin' awa,
Till they hear frae St Mungo's Cross Steeple again,
    The young ane gie vent tae his first canty craw.

And then they rush off tae their neebors an' freens,
    Wi' a bottle, and maybe a bannock, in han';
For this in their ain phraseology means,
    A twelve-month o' plenty whaurever they're gaun.

And quate, dacent fowk, in the deed o' the nicht,
  Are rudely awoke frae the slumber o' peace
Wi' the noise ower their heed, and are po'erless wi' fricht,
  While somebody shouts, 'Murder! murder! – Polece.'

And brithers curse brithers, a shockin' disgrace,
  But witless the heed's when the drap's in the e'e;
An' it's no the exception, but aften the case,
  That neeves, and whiles knives, end the 'first fittin'' spree.

How aften does sad-eyed Humanity greet
  At the pitiful tales frae the criminal cells
Which appear in the newspaper's recording sheet
  Of the ruin in homes where the drink-demon dwells?

While faithers and mithers their cronies will treat,
  Where the dram's measured oot for the price o' a saul,
Their bairnies are wandering aboot on the street,
  And sabbin' their herts oot wi' hunger and caul'.

I blush for those women so morally sunk,
  Though they're decent men's wives, and are decently clad,
That they're stretched on the pavement incapably drunk,
  While pure Ne'er-day pleasures may easy be had.

And a far sadder story we aften may read,
  Where a mother's been drunk when she gied tae her bed,
And laid ower her wean till she smothered it deed –
  How saut and how sober the tears she would shed.

And think what a number of 'bodies' are found
  In the Glasgow canals, and its river, the Clyde;
When ye've earnestly studied a list o' the drowned,
  How many were sober when 'gulphed in its tide?

Is'nt awfu' tae think that there's maist loss o' life,
  Maist sin and maist sorrow, maist drinking and crime,
When homely affections and joy should be rife,
  On the new-opened page o' the record o' time.

Jessie Russell, 1877

144

Ayrshire Jock

I, John Auld, in my garret here,
    In Sauchiehall Street, Glasgow, write,
Or scribble, for my writing-gear
    Is sadly worn: a dirty white
    My ink is watered to; and quite
Splay-footed is my pen – the handle
    Bitten into a brush; my light,
Half of a ha'penny tallow-candle.

A little fire is in the grate,
    Between the dusty bars, all red –
All black above: the proper state
    To last until I go to bed.
    I have a night-cap on my head,
And one smokes in a tumbler by me:
    Since heart and brain are nearly dead,
Who would these comforters deny me?

Ghosts lurk about the glimmering room,
    And scarce-heard whispers hoarsely fall:
I fear no more the rustling gloom,
    Nor shadows moving on the wall;
    For I have met at church and stall,
In streets and roads, in graveyards dreary,
    The quick and dead, and know them all:
Nor sight nor sound can make me eerie.

Midnight rang out an hour ago;
    Gone is the traffic in the street,
Or deadened by the cloak of snow
    The gallant north casts at the feet
    Of merry Christmas, as is meet;
With icicles the gutter bristles;
    The wind that blows now slack, now fleet,
In every muffled chimney whistles.

I'll draw the blind and shut – alas!
    No shutters here! . . . My waning sight
Sees through the naked window pass
    A vision. Far within the night
    A rough-cast cottage, creamy white,
With drooping eaves that need no gutters,
    Flashes its bronze thatch in the light,
And flaps its old-style, sea-green shutters.

There I was born. . . . I'll turn my back;
    I would not see my boyhood's days:
When later scenes my memories track,
    Into the magic pane I'll gaze.
    Hillo! the genial film of haze
Is globed and streaming on my tumbler:
    It's getting cold; but this I'll praise,
Though I'm a universal grumbler.

Now, here's a health to rich and poor,
    To lords and to the common flock,
To priests, and prigs, and – to be sure! –
    Drink to yourself, old Ayrshire Jock;
    And here's to rhyme, my stock and rock;
And though you've played me many a plisky,
    And had me in the prisoners' dock,
Here's my respects t'ye, Scottish whisky!

That's good! To get this golden juice
    I starve myself and go threadbare.
What matter though my life be loose?
    Few know me now, and fewer care.
    Like many another lad from Ayr –
This is a fact, and all may know it –
    And many a Scotchman everywhere,
Whisky and Burns made me a poet.

Just as the penny dreadfuls make
    The 'prentice rob his master's till,
Ploughboys their honest work forsake,
    Inspired by Robert Burns. They swill

146

Whisky like him, and rhyme; but still
Success attends on imitation
    Of faults alone: to drink a gill
Is easier than to stir a nation.

They drink, and write their senseless rhymes,
    Tagged echoes of the lad of Kyle,
In mongrel Scotch: didactic times
    In Englishing our Scottish style
    Have yet but scotched it: in a while
Our bonny dialects may fade hence:
    And who will dare to coin a smile
At those who grieve for their decadence?

These rhymesters end in scavenging,
    Or carrying coals, or breaking stones;
But I am of a stronger wing,
    And never racked my brains or bones.
    I rhymed in English, catching tones
From Shelley and his great successors;
    Then in reply to written groans,
There came kind letters from professors.

With these, and names of lords as well,
    My patrons, I brought out my book;
And – here's my secret – sold, and sell
    The same from door to door. I look
    My age; and yet, since I forsook
Ploughing for poetry, my income
    Comes from my book, by hook or crook;
So I have found the muses winsome.

That last rhyme's bad, the pun is worse;
    But still the fact remains the same:
My book puts money in my purse,
    Although it never brought me fame.
    I once desired to make a name,
But hawking daily an edition
    Of one's own poetry would tame
The very loftiest ambition.

Ah! here's my magic looking-glass!
    Against the panes night visions throng.
Lo! there again I see it pass,
    My boyhood! Ugh! The kettle's song
    Is pleasanter, so I'll prolong
The night an hour yet. Soul and body!
    There's surely nothing very wrong
In one more glass of whisky toddy!

John Davidson, *c.*1880

Springburn trams (William Graham) MITCHELL LIBRARY

from A Hundred Years Ago

A hundred years ago! As in a dream,
All things have changed along the human stream.
The thousand roaring wheels of traffic pass
Where the maids spread the linen on the grass;
The mighty ocean liners outward bound
Heave o'er the spot where windmill wheels went round.
The haystacks of the Trongate, where are they?
Where the green meadows which produced the hay?
Who were the last vain lovers (who can tell?)
That gazed beneath the alders at Arn's Well?
Oh! quaint arcadian city which appears
In the bright vista of a hundred years!
The ancient merchant in his scarlet cloak,
Grey wig and silver buckles, if he woke
From his archaic slumber, would he know
Th' Havannah of a century ago?
In that brave year of seventeen eighty-two
The stars looked out of smokeless heavens and knew
The city by its nine dim lamps. At dawn
The glimmering vapours from the bens were drawn,
And Lomond with a cheery face looked down
Through the clear morning on the thriving town.

William Canton, 1882

Construction of Prince's Dock, 1874
(Annan and Sons)
MITCHELL LIBRARY

Iron Shipbuilding on the Clyde

Ho, mates! go lay the keel-blocks down,
   And bring along the keel,
For we must build an iron ship,
   And that right off the reel;
And that right off the reel, my boys!
   With no faults to conceal,
Her frames of treble B – her shell
   Of 'Siemens-Martin's' steel.

For us the miner sinks the mine,
   For us the furnace glows;
For us Columbia's lofty pine
   Our rock-bound island knows;
Our rock-bound island knows, my boys!
   While o'er the heaving tide
Old India's famous teak is borne
   To Scotland and the Clyde.

Lay bar to bar, and butt to butt,
   And swing your hammers free,
See that no idle hands surround
   This virgin of the sea;
This virgin of the sea, my boys!
   For know, when she's afar,
The sailor's life is centred in
   Her weakest plate and bar.

Now see you follow fair, my lads,
   The draughtsman's deft design,
And shape with steady care, my lads,
   Each graceful curve and line;
Each graceful curve and line, my boys!
   For know we all with pride,

The ships are yet to build, my boys!
  To match those built on Clyde.

Bass Kennedy, 1888

Clyde shipbuilding, 1878 (*Great Industries of Great Britain*) MITCHELL LIBRARY

The Clyde

Ho! ye magnates of the city, study this unsavoury ditty,
  For it is a gruesome pity that such words I need inscribe;
But my love was slightly ailing, she desired a little sailing,
  And her wishes all prevailing, we embarked upon the Clyde.
But, alas! our noble river, how it made poor Nannie shiver,

Loud exclaiming, 'Oh, I never!' as her hanky stopped her nose,
For so fearful bad the stink was, and the water black as ink was,
   Just like Day & Martin's blacking, and as thick as Athole brose.

As we sat abaft the funnel, and were peering o'er the gunwale,
   Flew a queer bird oot the tunnel of a monster common sewer;
In his bill so long and taper seemed a dirty piece of paper,
   But he cut o'erhead a caper, and it fell beside me sure.
Now, as true's a duck's a diver, I declar'd it was a fiver
   That had travelled down the siver, and the bird brought to my side;
But in truth it was a sonnet, here's the words that were upon it:
   'To the Citizens of Glasgow, from the Genius of the Clyde.'

            Let Glasgow perish, should I plead in vain
            To thee, proud city! I, who gave thee birth,
            And suckled you through all the centuries?
            What gain although my banks uphold with pride
            The second city in an empire vast?
            Pollution-gorged, I heave in putrid form,
            A seething cesspool of a city's filth,
            In fermentation vile – contaminate.
            The hydra dire you've planted in my breast,
            Conceals a deadly foe with scorpion lash –
            A pestilential death-dispensing hell,
            More terrible than horror's wildest dream.
            Then, citizens, beware! cast off your apathy,
            And free from your vile filth your humble servant,
                                                    'CLYDE.'

'Guid preserve us a',' quo' Nannie, 'cast it frae ye, John, my mannie,
   For there's something isna cannie in that sable birdie's tale;'
'Na,' quo' I, 'in name o' thunner, wha wad write it, lass, I won'er?
   It's at ony rate a stunner, and I'll send it to the *Mail*.
For this smell a sow would scunner, and bring measles oot upon her,
   'Tis a blur on Scotland's honour, and a blot on Glasgow's pride;
It's to Providence defiance, it's to pestilence alliance,
   It's a sorry slur on science, and dishonour to the Clyde.'

Bass Kennedy, 1888

Doon the Watter at the Fair

Come listen tae me, Nannie dear,
   My cantie, tosh aul' wife,
We've stood for five an' thirty year
   The tussel an' the strife.
An' yearly as the time cam' roun',
   We never missed, I'm shair,
Tae spen' oor sair-won pastime doon
   The watter at the Fair.

Ye min' yon July morn langsyne,
   A rosy morn like this,
You pledged tae be for ever mine,
   An' sealed it wi' a kiss.
On board the *Petrel*, near Dunoon,
   Ye yielded tae my prayer,
An' aye sin' syne we've managed doon
   The watter at the Fair.

When you a snod mill lass, an' I
   A Brigton weaver chiel,
Then lad an' lass on deck did vie
   At rantin' jig or reel.
Aye tae the fiddler tint the tune,
   We danced the hin'maist pair,
An' took the brag frae a' gaun doon
   The watter at the Fair.

Sae haste an' bind yer siller hair,
   An' don your Paisley shawl,
We're still a cantie, couthie pair,
   The mair we're growin' aul'.
Though grey my locks an' bare my croon,
   An' you my frailties shair,
We'll taste again life's morn gaun doon
   The watter at the Fair.

The witchin' woodlan's waving green,
    An' bosky banks and braes
That fringe the bonnie Clyde, hae been
    Oor playgrun' a' oor days.
An' while the Maker hale an' soun'
    Is pleased oor lives tae spare,
We'll blithely trip thegither doon
    The watter at the Fair.

Sae haste ye, Nannie, come awa',
    An' dinna langsome be,
For thrangin' tae the Broomielaw,
    The focks gaun by wi' glee.
A twalmonth's toil in Glesca toun
    Is lichtsome, I declare,
Wi' twa-three days' diversion doon
    The watter at the Fair.

Bass Kennedy, 1888

Glasgow

Beautiful city of Glasgow, with your streets so neat and clean,
Your stately mansions, and beautiful Green!
Likewise your beautiful bridges across the river Clyde,
And on your bonnie banks I would like to reside.

    Chorus
    Then away to the West – to the beautiful West!
    To the fair city of Glasgow that I like the best,
    Where the river Clyde rolls on to the sea,
    And the lark and blackbird whistle with glee.

'Tis beautiful to see the ships passing to and fro,
Laden with goods for the high and the low;

So let the beautiful city of Glasgow flourish,
And may the inhabitants always find food their bodies to nourish.

The statue of the Prince of Orange is very grand,
Looking terror to the foe, with a truncheon in his hand,
And well mounted on a noble steed, which stands in the Trongate,
And holding up its foreleg, I'm sure it looks first-rate.

Then there's the Duke of Wellington's statue in Royal Exchange Square –
It is a beautiful statue I without fear declare,
Besides inspiring and most magnificent to view,
Because he made the French fly at the battle of Waterloo.

And as for the statue of Sir Walter Scott that stands in George's Square,
It is a handsome statue – few can with it compare,
And most elegant to be seen,
And close beside it stands the statue of Her Majesty the Queen.

Then there's the statue of Robert Burns in George Square,
And the treatment he received when living was very unfair;
Now, when he's dead, Scotland's sons for him do mourn,
But, alas! unto them he can never return.

Then as for Kelvin Grove, it is most lovely to be seen
With its beautiful flowers and trees so green.
And a magnificent water-fountain spouting up very high,
Where people can quench their thirst when they feel dry.

Beautiful city of Glasgow, I now conclude my muse,
And to write in praise of thee my pen does not refuse;
And, without fear of contradiction, I will venture to say
You are the second grandest city in Scotland at the present day!

William McGonagall, 1889

Ode to the Clyde

Hail, great black-bosomed mother of our city,
  Whose odoriferous breath offends the earth,
Whose cats and puppy dogs excite our pity,
  As they sail past with aldermanic girth!
No salmon hast thou in thy jet-black waters,
  Save what is adhering to the tins.
Thus thy adorers – Govan's lovely daughters –
  Adorn thy shrine with offerings for their sins.

No sedges check thy flow, nor water lily;
  Thy banks are unadorned with hip or haw,
'Cos why? – now, don't pretend you're *really* silly,
  There ain't no lilies at the Broomielaw.
MacBrayne defiles thy face with coaly sweepings,
  Into thy lap the tar expectorates;
The 'Caledonia's' cook his galley heapings
  Casts in thy face as if at one he hates.

Yet art thou great. Though strangers hold their noses
  When sailing down to Rothesay at the Fair,
Thy exiled sons would barter tons of roses
  To scent thy sweetness on the desert air.

Charles J. Kirk, 1910

Breathes There a Man–?

I sigh to be in Glesca just to hear the blackcock call
Beside the gloomy forests round the Rue de Sauchiehall,
To pull a bunch of heather off the breezy Broomielaw,
And chase the capercailzies down the glades of Kelvinhaugh.
In visions of Mount Vernon, with its bright eternal snow,
I've seen the homing eagles in the golden evening glow.
I yearn to see the pinnacles of classic Gilmorehill,
And stray through dewy Gorbals where the Nuts are hard nuts still.
There are rare deer in Strathbungo, very shy and swaddie-proof,
Who come a-ranging coyly from the shades of Crossmyloof.
Oh, my country! Oh, my kindred! Oh, my clachan on the Clyde!
I'm wearying to taste again the tarts of Kelvinside.
There are kelpies in the Kelvin, possils out in Possilpark,
In Bearsden the genus Ursus still pursues man for a lark;
Yet I'll brave these terrors, darling, for your sake time and again,
So you'll see me questing gaily up the scaurs of Rutherglen,
I shall come by Ecclefechan, by the Millgates of Millguy,
By Trongate dens and buts-and-bens, and Calton, too, ach ay!
You may hear my phlapping philabeg a-philabegging, lass,
As shanks' nag goes wolloping along the Schipka Pass.
So wait for me, my dearie, for your lusty man of war,
And you shall dine – eh – *table d'hote* in the halls of Grosvenor.

William J. F. Hutcheson, 1915

In Glasgow

(For F. G. Scott)

How can I but be fearful,
Who know not what I do
More than did they whose labours
We owe this chaos to?

I'd rather cease from singing,
Than make by singing wrong
An ultimate Cowcaddens,
Or Gorbals of a song.

I'll call myself a poet,
And know that I am fit
When my eyes make glass of Glasgow,
And foresee the end of it!

Hugh MacDiarmid, 1925

Symbol

Doun by the Clyde there is a skeleton
   That ne'er had a body: a ghost gaen deid
Afore it cam' alive. It micht hae won
   Its way, owre the world's waters, or the weed
O' time rax't abune it; nane then carin'
   Sin it had come through the storm o' the years:
But yon thing, neither a corp nor a bairn,
   Rots in the womb. Wha looks upon it peers
On mair than he sees – gin he but look richt:

Ayont they iron banes gang the Glasgow wynds
Fou o' sic skeletons, waesome tae the sicht
    That sklents unner the skulls an' meets the minds:
Day aftir day they walk owre Glasgow Green
    An' the wurds they speak are no' what the mouth
Speaks, but the een – an' ahint the een –
    Cryin', cryin': '*What hae ye dune tae oor youth?*'

William Soutar, 1932

Glasgow Street

Out of this ugliness may come
    some day so beautiful a flower
    that men will wonder at that hour
remembering smoke and flowerless slum
    and ask
            glimpsing the agony
    of the slaves who wrestle to be free
'But why were all the poets dumb?'

William Montgomerie, 1933

Industrial Scene

The women talk, tea-drinking by the fire
    In the back parlour. The rose afternoon
Stiffens out in the street to fog and mire.
    The blood-red bullying West confronts the moon.

The house-tops, sharpening, saw into the sky.
   Factory sirens wail and Rest is born,
A clockwork centipede that lumbering by
   Decorates heaven with silhouettes of horn.

Incandescent burners' arctic glare
   Strikes dead a thousand families as they sit
At high tea in the tenements. The air
   Takes at the tidal corner of the street

The hundred-horse-power pub's wave-shouldering boom
   And thickened voices babbling Judgment Day.
At the big house the Owner waits his doom
   While his Rhine-maiden daughters sit and play

Wagner and Strauss. Beneath the railway bridge
   In patient waxwork line the lovers stand.
Venus weeps overhead. Poised on the ridge
   The unemployed regard the Promised Land.

Edwin Muir, 1935

Glasgow, 1960

Returning to Glasgow after long exile
Nothing seemed to me to have changed its style.
Buses and trams all labelled 'To Ibrox'
Swung past packed tight as they'd hold with folks.
Football match, I concluded, but just to make sure
I asked; and the man looked at me fell dour,
Then said, 'Where in God's name are *you* frae, sir?
It'll be a record gate, but the cause o' the stir
Is a debate on "la loi de l'effort converti"
Between Professor MacFadyen and a Spanish pairty.'

I gasped. The newsboys came running along,
'Special! Turkish Poet's Abstruse New Song.
Scottish Authors' Opinions' – and, holy snakes,
I saw the edition sell like hot cakes!

Hugh MacDiarmid, 1935

Twin-Screw Set – 1902

Week after week I watched the darlings growing
Like two strange children in an orphan home,
Aft from the thrust block to the stop-valve throw-in,
Up from the bedplate to the L.P. dome.
One afternoon we swept the pit logs cleanly,
Set down a line of wedges, steel on wood,
Then laid the bedplate as you would a pin lay,
And saw the thing was good.

We squared it up and lined the eight great bearings;
Bedded the crankshaft down, and set up well
The eight box columns, and with plumbline fairings
Brought crosshead slides dead true and parallel.
We dropped connecting rods into their places
And bedded down the great big bottom ends;
Chipped oil grooves in the smooth whitemetal faces,
And felt they were our friends.

We faired the cylinders central and level,
Marked in the fitted bolts and screwed them tight;
Set the condenser, faced-up by 'The Devil',
One inch cast iron, and considered light.
We lined the pumps behind the L.P. columns,
And steam reverser, a new patent stunt;
Set starting gear and other what-d'ye-call-'ems
Upon the engine front.

The piston rods to pistons were adjusted,
The thrust shoes on their collars brought to bear;
Fixed lubricators with their dripper worsted,
Put balanced valves on the eccentric gear;
Connected pumps and tubed the big condenser,
Packed well its ferrules; and later the exhaust
Pipe pattern tried to place, so that its ends were
Cast true and nothing lost.

We set the valves; the bearing leads were taken,
The cleading fixed, and platforms laid in place;
Handrails and footplates put, and not a shake in
The whole arrangement from the top to base.
Survey them there, each one of them a beauty,
Five thousand H.P. on point six cut-off;
Designed for honest cross-Atlantic duty,
And each one looks a toff.

Take note of them; the crankshaft fourteen inches,
The L.P. cylinders are sixty-seven;
Stroke forty-eight; high-bred like all the princes,
An inspiration from the hosts of heaven.
The thrust is seven, all valve travels ditto,
The crosshead pin's diameter's the same;
Connecting rods at middle are a bit o'
That figure's sacred name.

The great propellers, shining like a sovereign,
Are seventeen feet diameter, three blades;
Seventy square feet of bronze on each shaft hovering
To push her through the currents and the trades.
They take their steam full bore about two-twenty,
The furnaces one hundred feet below
The funnel tops; and, fed with coal aplenty,
What care they if it blow!

William J. F. Hutcheson, 1937

The City Cemetery

(Written in Glasgow)

There are open railings and walls
and black earth and no trees and no grass
and wooden benches where old people sit
the whole afternoon without speaking.
All around there are tenements and shops.
The children play in streets and the trains
rattle past the graves. It is a poor district.

As if patching-up some piece of grey material, rain
-sodden rags hang across the windows.
The writing on the tombstones is unreadable, and anyway
for the last two hundred years they have been burying not men
but corpses without friends even to forget them, dead
secrets. But when the sun blazes for those few days
around June, surely the old bones down there feel something.

No leaf, no bird. Nothing but stone. Earth.
Is Hell like this? Pain and more pain, clamour,
misery, a chill that seeps everywhere freezing
everything; and the dead are not left in peace,
for life goes about its business here like a prostitute
who works only under the cover of darkness.

When the dirty evening twilight smears the sky
and the factory smoke falls back down
as grey ash, people are shouting in the pubs;
and then a train passes,
its echoes stretching the sounds like a trumpet's snarl.

– But not for Judgement Day. You have no names now,
so be at peace; if you can sleep, then sleep.
For even God may be forgetting you.

Luis Cernuda, *c.*1940, *translated by Ron Butlin*

Whose Children?

It was to the City of Glasgow you came,
Citizens who live and walk the streets here,
One and a half million of us,
Look on the flowing waters and the Cathedral
And proclaim the place Red City on the Clyde,
But you would not know, you who came to Glasgow,
You came and had gone before you had time to say Goodbye,
Only Good Morning. Ninety of you out of every thousand
Good Mornings – some did not wait to say Good Morning, Red City.
Never less than eighty out of the thousand
And only last year one hundred and eleven:
Ten thousand every five years,
Twenty thousand in ten years,
But you, you could not count up to about one.
The reek, the damp, the fog and the rotten walls,
Through which you came from God's Pearly Gates,
Choked you, and you could not say Goodbye, Red Clyde.
There was what the people called a smallpox epidemic
And half the City population queued up to get vaccinated:
What a racket before they, too, might have to say
Goodbye, dear Clyde.
And that cost twenty-five thousand pounds,
A heart-breaking rise on the rates and taxes
Of a half-penny in the pound,
And eight died. Eight out of one and a half million.
Mind you, if that smallpox had stopped the dogs,
The football play, and left the town short of Lord Provosts,
There would have been revolution.
But you would not know, you died,
Ninety out of every thousand
Not to grow up and become a doctor or a nurse,
A saint or college and university don
To plan and avenge –
So the fog and the damp and the rotten walls live on.

You are small, too small to hold a span of breath,
And the dogs, the football play, and the dance and Cathedral,
All proclaim the Red City on the Clyde.
Oh, the war, yes there is a war on,
A new kind of war it is called,
And the statesmen say what is most wanted now is population,
You ninety dead out of every thousand
Could not have considered that else you might have stayed here,
And there is no one to speak.
The damp, rotten walls, the soil and the fog,
Cannot argue against a four-ton bomb,
You never got a chance to make and throw a four-ton bomb,
You did not wait to see what statesmen can achieve
Through health and education,
Nor the accomplishments of people who make statesmen –
You did not stay with us.
And there is none to speak.
But I forget already: the dead of the RAF,
The Fleet and the Army speak grandly for you:
A better, new, wiser world they say to the open skies
And to the flames and the waters,
And the Civil Defence of the total war include you in their total.
The teachers of this great City are silent about you.
And the prophets leave the years to make this ugly poem:
Children and poetry ought to be lovely and sweet as lilac,
And the preacher says 'tis God's goodwill it should be so,
The Public Press knows what the Public does not want to know:
Murders, wars, brothels, divorces, dogs and racing,
All are ok front-page news – the Press knows –
To keep the civic mind and conscience innocent is silent.
The Police are too busy with sin and crime
And regulating traffic, too busy to notice you.
And should your little feet along the grandeur come
Of Sauchiehall Street –
But you will not do that in the finery and rich furs there,
Nor turn your little breasts, that could not hold life's breath,
Towards the sun.
The long miles of little feet and breathless breasts
Must not appear in the streets of the Red City on the Clyde.
So the citizens build miracle ships, and planes and greater bombs,

And the dance and show and centpercent goes on as the Public want.
Why did you not go to New Zealand?
To the meadows and the buttercups and daisies
And the clean sweet open spaces and laughter of children there:
Only two of you out of every thousand would have died
Away from the fog, the soil, the reek and rotten walls.
You little babes, Infant Mortality
That's what the Records name you.
Here is your epitaph: Out of every thousand births died
In 1938 – 87; 1939 – 80 (the lowest ever); 1940 – 95;
1941 – 111; 1942 – 90.
Looks and reads like a dog or racing card:
It is the birth and death of little babies in the Red City.
The poets cannot sing for you,
For you there is no song,
Your lullaby of fog and soil and damp and rotten walls
Would not make music even for the BBC,
And so the poets broke their lyres,
Only when the lyres lay dead did their music join your lullaby.
Whose children are you?
A magistrate of the Red City
Where Justice is not rationed writes this halting poem,
The rhythm of little feet and the laughter of little children
Are not here to pattern and shape a joyous song,
It is a halting poem of sin and shame and crime,
Convener of the Red Clyde Public Health writes this of you,
My children.

Edward Hunter, 1943

Glasgow from the south, *c.*1760 (Robert Paul) MITCHELL LIBRARY

from Setterday Nicht Symphonie

(Til Hugh MacDiarmid)

CITIE
Ay, luke on the citie, glitteran, braw,
birlan wi nicht on hir ain stane flair,
tynt i a traunce o glee-glentan een,
a spae-time o joy, a rapture o ease.
Ay, luke on the citie whaur she turns
time til a trumpet ti blare hir wull
bye aa blin losses, an cankeran cares,
an thochts thit rankle when anger is gane.
Ay, gaze on the citie, ma hert-felt freens!
Tak yuir full o a reel o bliss
an coonsil yuir herts ti lowp til the beat,
an whirl owre the waas thit stoppit yuir een
frae graupplan fair wi the mirk-mockan mune.

Oh wud ye be twintie an coortan a lass,
meltan hir sweirt weys doun wi yuir heat?
Or wud ye be fortie, an cantie, an boss
o the ploy wi the kimmers no awfu discreet?
Or wud ye leave age at the door o yuir hoose
an tak the hale range o the joys o the street,
keepan auld wi the auld,
an blye wi the teens,
admiran the bauld,
an chauntan wi weans?

Or hae ye a sorra deep doun i yuir breist,
turnan the warld til the shape o a face?
Then awa wi yuir pain til the week's-finish feast . . .
here's balm, an here's mercie, and infinite grace!
Birlan an whirlan an skirlan, ma joes . . .
the streets are upendan an tuiman the folk
oot o benches an kitchens an coonters, machines,
an lowsan thur lauchan ti lowp til the lift.

Ay, birl awa citie, mak a gob at the mune,
fling a haunfu o staurs owre the heids o the priests,
tak the Clyde i yuir airms an croon it a sang
o the ships need nae rivets ti mak them float weel.
Ay, whirl awa citie, ye've swat lang eneuch,
yuir week's wark huis made a braw tocher for some;
an nou here's the nicht lang prayed fur by aa,
anoyntit wi lauchter, sae sacrit til fun.
Ay, citie, ma citie, skirl awa citie,
screich oot yuir lauchan til waas faaan doun;
yuir flair is aa stampan wi lauds an wi lasses
wi joy i thur banes an daunce i thur bluid.
O citie, ma citie,
til freedom be leal!
Tak a haud o the nicht!
Wha's fur a quadrille?

                              *

The nicht's duin wi daunce, the citie's wabbit oot.
The mune's settlan doun i the lap o the lift.
The folk ur aa skailan frae screen-ploy an pub
an gaean thur weys til sleep an til dwaum.
The nicht's duin wi daunce, ootstreicht on the flair;
the citie is dowsan the gems i hir goun.
Ay, luke on the citie whaur she sleeps
wi luve on hir conscience an truth in hir airms,
wi ease i hir banes an weirds i hir bluid.
The staurs sclim the lift, burn brichter an brichter;
the universe birls on its lang solemn wey.
Ay, sleep awa citie, ma douce smilan citie,
gaither strength fur the morn an the morn furbye,
an be it a daurk daw, or be it a bricht daw,
be it rain, be it sleet, be it bleezard wi claws,
yuir Setterday's lauchan wull ding doun the deils
that lowp frae the stanes as men bigg thur roads.
Ay, sleep awa citie, ma douce raucle citie,
sleep weel an sleep deep
wi yuir mirk-mockan een.

John Kincaid, 1948

A Glesca Rhapsodie

(for Thurso Berwick)

Eh, ma citie o raucle sang,
ma braid stane citie wi dwaums o steel.
Eh, ma Glesca, ma mither o revolt,
dauran the wunds o time in a raggit shawl.
Eh ma hanselt hinnie wi scaurs o war,
ma twalmonth lassock, ma carlin ages auld.

Chaunt me a rummlan neerday mass,
intone me psalms o bairnies in backcoorts,
sing me the setterdays thit staucher owre
the dreich cauld wecht o the waerife weeks.
Pipe me a reel o tapsiltoorie days
ti swing about the langerie the lums weel ken;
eh, fife me halloweens ti bigg a brig
atween the keenin grey o slumtith's lear
an yon douce lauchin o oor Glesca spirit;
dirl me strathspeys o tenement an shielin
ti gar the saul gae lowpan crottlan waas;
an whussle a jig o puirtith full wi praties,
an crood me ceilidhs in a luver's close
sae I may fuit a sermon duin in daunce
atween the dounset creeds aa skailed o faith.

Ma hinnie lauchs wi drowie een
an fulls me fou o glaumerie.
She pairts the flichteran haar o efternuin
an tittles luve atween twa watergaws,
an glinks o wudrife gleid ablow the hert.
She braks the fairheid fronds o Kelvingrove
ti mell an incense fur oor lemanrie,
an tuims me oot the daurk-douce wines o Clyde
ti pent oor warsslan wi reid gaietie.
Ma hinnie is no lassock no yet stappit,
fur hunger kennt hir ploy an age afore

she drappt the ugsom factries frae hir wame;
an puirtith, aye hir gallivantin man,
huis gaed his gait gey aften, speiran wark,
an left hir lourd an lane in labour,
ti dree ane routh o street-begrutten weans;
an hirplan daith huis bairned her mony times
i the smouchteran steer o a wheen o wars.
— But eh ma hinnie, ma raucle hizzie,
ma hinnie o syvers rinnin wi lear,
ma limmer o tenements bydan fur daw,
ma skilp o skelps frae a reuch-rife warld,
ma besom blye wi glinkan een,
I rise frae yuir mou wi ma saul ondaunsin
an a solemn sang i ma swoundan hert.

Scart ma een wi fingers o steel
suld I gae greinan fur the derelict staurs
yet be beukieburd-blin til syver-schene,
til raucle mystery i puirtith's een,
an warld onfechtan i ma causey scaurs.

Brak ma banes wi hauns o steel
suld I mak gods wha kenna wardlin stour
an flee til them fur tawpie toom remeid.
Ir suld I clash o hevins wi the deid
an seek but them — lat there be nae retour.

Gralloch me oot wi airms o steel
suld Gorbals lauchter dwine i ma reithe hert,
suld I be fause til tenement an fiere,
an lang ti grow aa siller-sonsie, steir,
by thowless practice o the Monger's airt.

But luke . . .
Camlachie stalks across the firmament
ti licht a gleid against aa tyrannie,
an Brigton braks the tap o trauchled yerth
to lay doun shairer founds fur dwaums,
an Garngad shaws its Shannon treesyur
ti pey its bairnies fur a wake fur beautie.

Ay, luke . . .
ma hinnie citie streetches in the daw
ti tak the sun's heich routh o glaumerie
an mell it wi the reek, the yairds o Clyde,
the tenements, the haas, an kirks, an lums,
sae keltic leids can grow in puirtith streets.
An heich ma hinnie throws hir lauchin vyce
ayont the mysteries o lowerin lyfts
ti full hir luvers wi hir certaintie.

Eh ma hinnie o raucle sang,
ma braid stane citie wi dwaums o steel,
ma hanselt hinnie, ma carlin gurlie-rife,
ma douce reithe citie, ma haill lee-life.

John Kincaid, 1948

News of the World

As I came round by Templeton's
The sun was sliding low,
And every spire round Glasgow Green
Gave off its godly glow.

Deep in its rut the river shed
A skin of shit and scum,
And glinted through the fretted bridge,
Gold as Byzantium.

Then suddenly the sun was snuffed
Behind a sooty cloud,
And night let fall on Glasgow Green
Its sulphur-stinking shroud.

Black in its bed the river slinks
Down to the whining weir.
The yellow lamps along its banks
Come out – and with them, fear.
And fear floods out and fills the dark,
And the dark and the fear are one,
And standing on this bridge I know
The things that must be done.

For hardly fifty yards from here
Last night at half-past-ten
A Southside girl was gagged and shagged
By seven Brigton men.
And when the bully-boys were done,
They left her on the mud:
A crumpled stem and a crushed flower
And a dark splash of blood.

The slimy river secretly
Slid on, and far away
A furnace flared into the night
And the night was light as day.
A whistle shrilled. Across the Green
To London Road the men
Ran stumbling, and to hide their flight
The darkness dropped again.

But torchlight sliced the darkness where
She lay limp on the mud.
A crushed flower and a crumpled stem
And a dark splash of blood.
And torchlight fell on the twisted face
And it fell on the tangled hair.
On the clawed thighs, on the clenched fists
The torches threw their glare.
And then big Sean of Surrey Street
Came knifelike through the crowd,
And when he knew that it was true
He swore by holy blood
That he would hunt the bastards down

Had dibbled dirty seed,
And all their cheeks would grin like lips
And every throat would bleed.

Aye, well might the stinking river sink
As though in fear it fell.
And well might the rising sun burn red
As though it rose on hell.
For thirteen Southside men had sworn
To smear their blades with blood
For the crumpled stem and the crushed flower
And the red stain on the mud.

And now as I stand on the swaying bridge
Above the sluggish stream,
I know that a night of knives is down
And I know it is no dream.
My fingers clutch the greasy rail,
Frozen fast by fear.
A minute from the clanging street,
And yet I cannot stir.
And faint and far across the Green
To the grimy banks of Clyde
From the depths of the dark there twists a scream
Like a slow sword in the side.
Cry upon cry, and the crying rises,
Falls, and swells again,
And nearer, louder beat the drumming
Feet of running men,
Till close at hand the thud of feet
Is stilled. The shouting dies.
The furnace flares. The killing ground
Is framed beneath my eyes.

At the place on the path where it was done
Last night at half-past-ten,
Their blades ablaze like liquid light
Are seven Brigton men.

They stand like a glinting rock on the shore
As the tide creeps all around –

Thirteen crouching Southside men
Who move without a sound.

And they close on the men who stand on the spot
Where she lay sprawled on the mud.
A crumpled petal, a crushed stem,
And a dark splash of blood.

Is it only fear that holds me here
Where I stand on the bridge alone,
Though I know how a blade can slice as though
Through blubber to the bone?

A twisted face and tangled hair
And clawed thighs on the mud.
A crumpled stem and a crushed flower
And a dark splash of blood.

And a shaking scream from a broken boy
Is signal for the shock.
Cry upon cry. With a flashing surge
The sea is upon the rock.
A chalky face is crossed with red,
And again, again, again.
Behind the savage glitter of
A filed and flailing chain,
I see a boy go down on his back,
His muffler running red,
While the kid who killed him falls beside
Him, gashed across the head.

The furnace flames are curling low
And the dark returns at last,
And through the scream of fighting shrills
A piercing whistle blast.
And darkness drops on the Green again
And I move like a man in a dream –
A dream of hell – but knowing well
That things are what they seem.

Is there a man who never knew
A red mist mask his sight?
Is there a man who never knew
The joy I knew tonight?

As I came round by Templeton's
The sun was sliding low.
In a black night of black despair
From Glasgow Green I go.

Iain Hamilton, 1949

Perishin' Poem

Winter's came,
The snow has fell,
Wee Josis nosis frozis well,
Wee Josis frozis nosis skintit
Winter's diabolic – intit?

Bud Neill, 1952

Maxwell Park (George Oliver)

The Labour Provost

Air – *The White Cockade*

When I was young and fu' o' fire
Tae smash the Tories was my firm desire

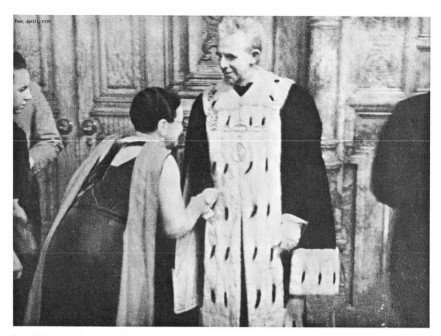

Lord Provost Dollan welcomes guests at a civic reception, 1939 (*Picture Post*) MITCHELL
LIBRARY

But noo I'm auld I ha'e mair sense
I just blame the lot on Providence.

Chorus:
I am a man o' high degree
Lord Provost o' this great cittee
The workers want a world tae gain
But I'm content wi' my badge and chain.

Wi' John Maclean and Willie Gallacher
Yince I thocht I micht ha'e travelled far
But noo the thocht, it fairly makes me pale
Wanst I landed in Barlinnie Jail!

Wi' ma ermine coat and my office seal
For Socialism I am fu' o' zeal

The principles of socialism are a' very well
Bit ye mustnae forget tae look after yersel.

Let the Russians bum aboot their five-year plans
Their tractors, factories and Hydro dams
Lang afore thae Bolshies had an ounce o' skill
We up and nationalised old Barnhill.

Lang afore the Poles or Rumanians
The Czechoslovaks or Bulgarians
We led the workers on tae victorie
We municipalised the Govan Ferree.

So whan the Queen cam's tae see us a'
Republican sentiments we'll banish awa'
On bended knee, or if it suits,
On hunkers doon we'll lick her boots.

Iain Nicolson, *c*.1955

Ibrox, *c*.1956 (George Oliver)

Sràid ann an Glaschu

Tha uinneagan glana nam prìosan fosgailt,
is cailleachan tiugha a' leigeil an anail,
am broillich aig fois, 's an tea seachad;
a' còmhradh 's a' bruidhinn, air prìs an ime,
is cò tha pòsadh, is cò fhuair piseach,
air àrdachadh màil, is aodach, is nithean
a thachair an dè air chùl nam balla.

Air an t-sràid a-muigh tha a' chlann a' ruideil,
fear a' tilleadh on bhùth, 's tè a' cùnntadh chlachan,
an lomnochd còmhdaicht' le òige 's cion cleachdaidh,
's an sùilean gorm fo chlàbar eachdraidh.

Na mnathan òga le 'n aparain flùrach
a' còmhradh ri chèile bho uinneig gu uinneig,
is fìon na fala gan cumail fallain,
saor o uallach ach airgead is daorach,
is, theagamh, eagal cus chloinne a ghiùlain.

Na fir nan seasamh nan lèintean a' bruidhinn
air eich, ball-coise is bocsairean cliùiteach,
fear chaidh a mhurt, is Jane Russell,
is iomadach cuspair cudthromach eile:
cha laigh smal air na h-inntinnean dripeil
tha cnuasachd na beatha-s' o bhracaist gu suipeir.

'Se grian foghair is saorsainn feasgair
a chruinnich na blàthan daonda cneasd seo
air sràid anmoch am baile Ghlaschu
goirid mum facas na speuran laiste.

Street in Glasgow

The clean windows of the prisons are open,
and fat old women are taking their ease,
with bosoms at peace, and tea over;
yarning and talking of the price of butter,
and who's to marry, and who has a baby,
the raising of rents, and clothes, and what
happened yesterday behind the walls.

Out on the street the children are playing,
a boy's back from the shop, a girl counts chuckies,
youth and simplicity cover their bareness,
and their eyes are blue under history's mire.

The young women, with their floral aprons,
talk together from window to window,
while the wine of the blood keeps them healthy,
free from cares, but for money and boozing,
and, perhaps, the fear of too frequent childbirth.

The men in their shirt-sleeves stand discussing
horses and football and notable boxers,
the recent murder, and Jane Russell,
and many another weighty subject:
no gloom lies on the active minds
that consider life, from breakfast to supper.

An autumn's sun and an evening's leisure
brought out these human, kindly blossoms
on a late street in the city of Glasgow,
shortly before the sky was seen burning.

Ruaraidh MacThómais (Derick Thomson), 1956

Glasgow Beasts, an a Burd haw, an Inseks, an, aw, a Fush

(Tae Shimpei Kusano)

see me
wan time
ah wis a fox
an wis ah sleekit! ah
gaed slinkin

        heh

an snappin

        yeh

the blokes
aa sayed ah wis a GREAT fox
aw nae kiddin
ah wis pretty good
had a whole damn wood
in them days
hen

An wan time
ah wis a moose
a richt wee douce
chap
Maw
kep sayin
haw
hint
it
awful
an
it's
aa
a
trap

chums
this time
ah wis a bed–bug
Dostoevsky
yelly caurs
cawd
Haw Desire
an
here wee me

        an wance
        ah wis a zebra
        heh heh
        crossin

        syne
anither
        ah wis a midgie
time
        neist a stank
ah wis a
        foon that kin o
minnie
        thankless
aw
        didjye
the pond
        ever
haw
        spen
the shoogly caur
        a
gaun
        hail simmer
see s
        stottin
a frond
        up
fir
        an
ma wee jaur
        doon

Hooch
a heilan coo
wis mair liker
it
   the hiker
s
hoo hoos
ferr feart
o ma
herr–do

honess
pals
like
no been born
a cleg
s e bess

ho
it wis a laugh
been
a giraffe like
ma neck
goat sneckit
in this tree
so ah says
haw Sara
an she says whit
way ur ye staunin
aa bandy–leggit?
bandy–leggit
ah says
so help me
get
yir
giraffe
free

an wance
ah wis a budgie
  like
Wee Davie
123
Garscadden Road
(oot Polmadie)

come back
as a coal-hoarse
ho the

        heavy

an
hauf the day
wi yir piece
hauf-etten
hung
roon yir
ear

Ian Hamilton Finlay, 1961

Cod Liver Oil and Orange Juice

It was oot o the east there came a hard man
Aw haw, aa the wey fae Brigton

> *Chorus*
> *Ah-ha, Glory Hallelujah,*
> *The cod liver oil and the orange juice.*

He went intae a pub and he came oot paraletic,
Aw haw, the VP and the cider.

Does this bus go tae the Denny-Palais,
Aw haw, Ah'm lookin fur a lumber.

In the Palais he met Hairy Mary
Aw haw, the floer o the Calton.

He says tae her, Tell me hen are ye dancin?
Aw naw, it's jist the wey Ah'm staunin.

He says tae her, You're wan in a million.
Aw haw, so's your chances.

Can Ah run ye hame Ah've goat a pair o sannies.
Aw haw, you're helluva funny.

Up the back close and doon the dunny
Aw naw, it wisnae fur the first time.

Her maw came oot tae go tae the didgy
Aw haw, he buggered off sharpish.

She tried tae find the hard man, he's jined the Foreign Legion
Aw haw, Sahara and the camels.

So Hairy Mary had a little baby,
Aw haw, its faither's in the army.

Carl MacDougall, 1962

King Billy

Grey over Riddrie the clouds piled up,
dragged their rain through the cemetery trees.
The gates shone cold. Wind rose
flaring the hissing leaves, the branches
swung, heavy, across the lamps.
Gravestones huddled in drizzling shadow,

flickering streetlight scanned the requiescats,
a name and an urn, a date, a dove
picked out, lost, half regained.
What is this dripping wreath, blown from its grave
red, white, blue, and gold
'To Our Leader of Thirty years Ago' –

Bareheaded, in dark suits, with flutes
and drums, they brought him here, in procession
seriously, King Billy of Brigton, dead,
from Bridgeton Cross: a memory of violence,
brooding days of empty bellies,
billiard smoke and a sour pint,
boots or fists, famous sherrickings,
the word, the scuffle, the flash, the shout,
bloody crumpling in the close,
bricks for papish windows, get
the Conks next time, the Conks ambush
the Billy Boys, the Billy Boys the Conks till
Sillitoe scuffs the razors down the stank –
No, but it isn't the violence they remember
but the legend of a violent man
born poor, gang-leader in the bad times
of idleness and boredom, lost in better days,
a bouncer in a betting club,
a quiet man at last, dying
alone in Bridgeton in a box bed.
So a thousand people stopped the traffic
for the hearse of a folk hero and the flutes
threw 'Onward Christian Soldiers' to the winds
from unironic lips, the mourners kept
in step, and there were some who wept.

Go from the grave. The shrill flutes
are silent, the march dispersed.
Deplore what is to be deplored,
and then find out the rest.

Edwin Morgan, 1963

Glasgow Green

Clammy midnight, moonless mist.
A cigarette glows and fades on a cough.
Meth-men mutter on benches,
pawed by river fog. Monteith Row
sweats coldly, crumbles, dies
slowly. All shadows are alive.
Somewhere a shout's forced out – 'No!' –
it leads to nothing but silence,
except the whisper of the grass
and the other whispers that fill the shadows.

'What d'ye mean see me again?
D'ye think I came here jist for that?
I'm no finished with you yet.
I can get the boys t'ye, they're no that faur away.
You wouldny like that eh? Look there's no two ways aboot it.
Christ but I'm gaun to have you Mac
if it takes all night, turn over you bastard
turn over, I'll –'
                Cut the scene.
Here there's no crying for help,
it must be acted out, again, again.

This is not the delicate nightmare
you carry to the point of fear
and wake from, it is life, the sweat
is real, the wrestling under a bush
is real, the dirty starless river
is the real Clyde, with a dishrag dawn
it rinses the horrors of the night
but cannot make them clean,
though washing blows
                where the women watch
by day,

and children run,
     on Glasgow Green.

And how shall these men live?
Providence, watch them go!
Watch them love, and watch them die!
How shall the race be served?
It shall be served by anguish
as well as by children at play.
It shall be served by loneliness
as well as by family love.
It shall be served by hunter and hunted in their endless chain
as well as by those who turn back the sheets in peace.
The thorn in the flesh!
Providence, water it!
Do you think it is not watered?
Do you think it is not planted?
Do you think there is not a seed of the thorn
as there is also a harvest of the thorn?
Man, take in that harvest!
Help that tree to bear its fruit!
Water the wilderness, walk there, reclaim it!
Reclaim, regain, renew! Fill the barns and the vats!

Longing,
  longing
    shall find its wine.

Let the women sit in the Green
and rock their prams as the sheets
blow and whip in the sunlight.
But the beds of married love
are islands in a sea of desire.
Its waves break here, in this park,
splashing the flesh as it trembles
like driftwood through the dark.

Edwin Morgan, 1963

'glasgow's full of artists'

glasgow's full of artists
they're three feet tall
and eat sherbet dabs

Alan Jackson, 1965

Six Glasgow Poems

I   THE GOOD THIEF

heh jimmy
yawright ih
stull wayiz urryi
ih

heh jimmy
ma right insane yirra pape
ma right insane yirwanny uz jimmy
see it nyir eyes
wanny uz

heh

heh jimmy
lookslik wirgonny miss thi gemm
gonny miss thi GEMM jimmy
nearly three a cloke thinoo

dork init
good jobe they've gote thi lights

2 SIMPLE SIMON

thurteen bluddy years wi thim ih
no even a day aff
jiss gee im thi fuckin heave
weeks noatiss nur nuthin
gee im thi heave
thats aw

ahll tellyi sun
see if ah wiz Scot Symon
ahd tell thim wherrty stuff their team
thi hole fuckin lota thim
thats right

a bluddy skandal thats whit it iz
a bluddy skandal

sicken yi

3 COLD, ISN'T IT

wirraw init thigithir missyz
geezyir kross

4 A SCREAM

yi mist yirsell so yi did
we aw skiptwirr ferz njumptaffit thi lights
YIZIR AW PINE THEY FERZ THIMORRA
o it wizza scream
thaht big shite wiz dayniz nut

tellnyi jean
we wirraw shoutn backit im
rrose shoutit shi widny puhllit furra penshin
o yi shooda seeniz face
hi didny no wherrty look

thing iz tay
thirz nay skool thimorra
thi daft kunt wullny even getiz bluddy ferz

5 THE MIRACLE OF THE BURD AND THE FISHES

ach sun
jiss keepyir chin up
dizny day gonabootlika hawf shut knife
inaw jiss cozzy a burd

luvur day yi
ach well
gee it a wee while sun
thirz a loat merr fish in thi sea

6 GOOD STYLE

helluva hard tay read theez init
stull
if yi canny unnirston thim jiss clear aff then
gawn
get tay fuck ootma road

ahmaz goodiz thi lota yiz so ah um
ah no whit ahm dayn
tellnyi
jiss try enny a yir fly patir wi me
stick thi bootnyi good style
so ah wull

Tom Leonard, 1967

The Coming of the Wee Malkies

Whit'll ye dae when the wee Malkies come,
if they dreep doon affy the wash-hoose dyke,
an pit the hems oan the sterrheid light,
an play wee heidies oan the clean close-wa,
an bloo'er yir windae in wi the baw,
missis, whit'll ye dae?

Whit'll ye dae when the wee Malkies come,
if they chap yir door an choke yir drains,
an caw the feet fae yir sapsy weans,
an tummle thur wulkies through yir sheets,
an tim thur ashes oot in the street,
missis, whit'll ye dae?

Whit'll ye dae when the wee Malkies come,
if they chuck thur screwtaps doon the pan,
an stick the heid oan the sanit'ry man;
when ye hear thum shauchlin doon yir loaby,
chantin, 'Wee Malkies! The gemme's a bogey!'
– Haw, missis, whit'll ye dae?

Stephen Mulrine, 1967

Whitevale, 1966 (Robert Walker)

191

The Jeely Piece Song

I'm a skyscraper wean; I live on the nineteenth flair,
But I'm no' gaun oot tae play ony mair,
'Cause since we moved tae Castlemilk, I'm wastin' away
'Cause I'm gettin' wan meal less every day:

> *Chorus*
> *Oh ye cannae fling pieces oot a twenty-storey flat,*
> *Seven hundred hungry weans'll testify to that.*
> *If it's butter, cheese or jeely, if the breid is plain or pan,*
> *The odds against it reaching earth are ninety-nine tae wan.*

Back court (George Oliver)

On the first day ma maw flung oot a daud o' Hovis broon;
It came skytin' oot the windae and went up insteid o' doon.
Noo every twenty-seven hoors it comes back intae sight
'Cause ma piece went intae orbit and became a satellite.

On the second day ma maw flung me a piece oot wance again.
It went and hut the pilot in a fast low-flying plane.
He scraped it aff his goggles, shouting through the intercom,
'The Clydeside Reds huv goat me wi' a breid-an-jeely bomb.'

On the third day ma maw thought she would try another throw.
The Salvation Army band was staunin' doon below.
'Onward, Christian Soldiers', was the piece they should've played
But the oompah man was playing a piece an' marmalade.

We've wrote away to Oxfam to try an' get some aid,
An' a' the weans in Castlemilk have formed a 'piece brigade'.
We're gonnae march to George's Square demanding civil rights
Like nae mair hooses ower piece-flinging height.

Adam McNaughtan, 1967

Glasgow, Easter 1968

I hate this city
and I reject it.
Love for it has tired
me out. The good
I expected when
I was a child has
been slaughtered at
every week's end.
Even a woman here
has to grow manly.

There is no gentle
place for a woman here.
It is a land of wee
hard men and all I
am wanted for is to
stand and cheer.
There is a service
to provide the
bandages.
I hate this city
and I reject it.

Joan Ure, 1968

Glasgow

1.

Betty's Bar the Ship Inn
Dick's Bar the Dublin Vaults

Saturday night, the Broomielaw
pink papers flutter at the corners

like exotic birds

2.

Queen's dock on a Sunday morning
a noisy bevy of drunken gulls

the pier lined with pungent barrels
of sourmash bourbon whiskey

from Louisville, Kentucky, USA

3.

Thick fog over the docks
and as thick a silence

only one name of a ship
lit by green light

Sunrana, Kristiansand

Kenneth White, 1968

the docks on Sunday

        Hulks, ruined warehouses
echo the blasting radio from the hammer-tin
place across the estuary
The grasses blow, send their purple and white
crestfeathers floating
        Sunny SUNDAY
        Water moving, and I too
in imagined movement
        THINGS
        cold and bitter smell
of roasted iron and squashed boxes
     rusty tins, bed springs
shadow on the mulchy peat
        NOISE
        seagull cry.
The two walk on the dirty shore, crunch.
Blue trains run, clatters and squealing
        bus brakes
CRACKING corrugated tin SHATTERING
foottrodden glass

         waste dockland
Bagpipes shriek past the ricket remains of
wooden watchtowers, deserted tunnel domes
where glass was punched out and flowers float
out . . . out . . . out . . . out . . .

Jean Milton, 1969

Rider

i

a grampus whacked the hydrophone / Loch Fyne left its green bed,
    fled / shrieking to Cowal / it all began
the nutcracker closed round Port Glasgow / it snapped with a burst
    of docks and / capstans downwind like collarstuds
cabbage whites in deadlock / were hanged from geans and rowans /
    wedlock-red
Greenock in steam / hammered albatrosses onto packingcases / without
    forgiveness / zam
by the waters of Glasgow / angels hung pilgrims, primroses, Dante,
    black blankets / over and over / the acid streams
a giant hedgehog lifting the Necropolis / solid silver / to the moon /
    sang of the deluge
long keys of gas unlocked the shaking Campsies at / last, at least /
    four drumlins were heard howling / as far as Fenwick Moor
Calderpark was sucked into a belljar, came out / at Kalgoorlie with
    elephants and northern lights
ravening taxis roasted dogs in basements, basted / chicken wheels in
    demolition oil / slept by the swing / of the wrecker's ball
the Holy Loch turned to granite chips, the ships / died with their
    stiff upper lips reaching to Aviemore
Para Handy sculled through the subway with the Stone of Destiny /
    shot the rapids at Cessnock right into Sunday morning

a coelacanth on stilts was setting fire to Sauchiehall Street when Tom
    Leonard /
sold James B. V. Thomson a horse, black /
in the night and dust / which galloped him away /
deep as the grave / writing

ii

Davidson looked through the telescope at MacDiarmid and said / what,
    is that God
Davidson rode off on a blood-splashed stag / into the sea / horses
    ultimately
Davidson sold / fish to Neptune, fire / to Prometheus, to himself /
    a prisoner's iron bed, the red
sun rose flapping slowly over Nietzsche / bars melted into sand /
    black marias stalled in Calton
the rainbow dropped its pot of lead on Peterhead / the peter keys
    were blown to breadcrumbs, fed
to men forbid / the men bought lead, built jails, went mad, lay dead /
    in iron fields
the jaws of Nero smouldered in a dustbin / cinders tingled / the dead
    rose / tamam
sulphur shoes dancing to Mars / their zircon eyeshades flashed,
    beryllium / toeguards clipped Mercury's boulders
Lucretius was found lying under the flary walls / of a universe in the
    Crab nebula / crying
the dancers brought him water / where he lay he rose, froze / in a
    mandala like a flame / blessing
the darkness of all disbelievers / filaments of the Crab wrapped him
    in hydrogen shroud / remade
he walked by Barrhead and Vauxhall Bridge, by the sea waited / with
    his dark horse in the dangerous night air
for a rider / his testament
delivered to the earth, kicking /
the roots of things

iii

five hundred million hummingbirds sat in the Kelvin Hall / three
    hundred thousand girls took double basses

in a crocodile to Inverkip / six thousand children drew Rothesay
    through twelve thousand kites / two hundred
plumbers with morning cellos galvanized the bedmakers of Fairlie /
    forty babies
threw their teething-rings at a helicopter / trickety-track / till
    Orpheus looked back
and there was nothing but the lonely hills and sky unless the chilling
    wind was something / and the space
of pure white pain where his wife had held his hand from hell / he
    left the place
and came to a broken shack at midday / with carts and horses /
    strong dark ragged boys
played in the smoke / the gypsies gave him soup and bread / for the
    divine brooch / who cares
what is divine, he said / and passed into the valley of the Clyde,
    a cloud / followed
and many campfires in that landscape, dogs whining, cuckoos,
    glasshouses, thundershowers /
David Gray shook the rain from his hair and held his heart, the
    Luggie flashed
in the lightning of the last March storm / he led a sweet brown mare
    into the mist / the apple-boughs
closed over, where the flute
of Orpheus was only wished for /
in the drip of trees

iv

butcher-boys tried to ward off sharks / the waters rose quickly /
    great drowned bankers
floated from bay-windows / two housemaids struggled on Grosvenor
    Terrace with a giant conger
the Broomielaw was awash with slime and torn-out claws and
    anchor-flakes / rust and dust
sifted together where a dredger ploughed up the Gallowgate / pushed a
    dirty wave over Shettleston
spinning shopfronts crashed in silence / glassily, massively /
    porticoes tilting / settled in mud
lampreys fastened on four dead sailors drifting through Finnieston /
    in a Drygate attic

James Macfarlan threw his pen at the stinking wall / the whisky and
    the stinking poverty
ran down like ink / the well of rats was bottomless and Scotch / the
    conman and the conned
fought on / the ballads yellowed, the pubs filled / at Anderston he
    reached his grave in snow / selah
the ruined cities were switched off / there was no flood / his father
    led a pedlar's horse
by Carrick fields, his mother sang / the boy rode on a jogging back /
    far back / in rags /
Dixon's Blazes roared and threw more poets in its molten pools /
    forges on fire
matched the pitiless bread, the head
long hangdog, the lifted elbow /
the true bloody pathos and sublime

v

Kossuth took a coalblack horse from Debrecen / clattered up
    Candleriggs into the City Hall
three thousand cheers could never drown the groaning fortress-
    bars / a thousand years
heard the wind howl / scimitars, eagles, bugles, edicts, whips,
    crowns, in the pipes / playing / the grave plain in the sun
handcuffed keelies shouted in Albion Street / slogans in red
    fragments broke the cobblestones, Kossuth
drew a mirage on electric air / the hare sat calmly on the
    doorstep / it was Monday over all the world / om
Tom McGrath mixed bread and milk for the young hare / Monk and
    Parker spoke in a corner / the still room
was taken / Dougal Graham stood on his hands, the bell / rang
    between his feet / he rolled
on his hump through the swarming Tontine piazzas, swam / in dogs,
    parcels, puddles, tobacco-quids
ran with a bawbee ballad five feet long / felt fishwives / gutted
    a brace of Glasgow magistrates / lay
with a pig in his arms and cried the city fathers bitches / till
    a long shadow fell on pedlars
and far away the sound of hoofs / increased in moonlight / whole
    cities crouched in saddlebags

churches, dungeons, juntas dangled from reins / like grasses
    picked from the rank fields
and drops of halter sweat
burned men to the bone, but the hare
like mad / played

Edwin Morgan, 1969

The Butchers of Glasgow

The butchers of Glasgow have all got their pride
But they'll tell you that Willie's the prince
For Willie the butcher he slaughtered his wife
And he sold her for mutton and mince

It's a terrible story to have to be telt
And a terrible thing to be done
For what kind of man is it slaughters his wife
And sells her a shilling a pun

For lifting his knife and ending her life
And hanging her high like a sheep
You widnae object but you widnae expect
He wid sell the poor woman so cheap

But the Gallowgate folk were delighted
It didnae cause them any tears
They swore that Willie's wife Mary
Was the best meat he'd sold them for years

Matt McGinn, 1969

Glasgow

City, cauldron of a shapeless fire,
bubbling with brash Irish and a future

that stares from fifteen stories towards the Clyde.
The cotton and tobacco plants have died

Plantation St is withered. You love your ships,
hate your police, in whisky-coloured sleeps

adore your footballers. Victoria's not amused
at Celtic Park or Ibrox where the horsed

dice-capped policeman, seared by pure flame
trot in white gauntlets round your serious game

and the roaring furnaces bank your last pride.
They shed the rotting tenements flying goalward.

Iain Crichton Smith, 1969

You Lived in Glasgow

You lived in Glasgow many years ago.
I do not find your breath in the air.
It was, I think, in the long-skirted thirties
when idle men stood at every corner
chewing their fag-ends of a failed culture.
Now I sit here in George Square

where the War Memorial's yellow sword glows bright
and the white stone lions mouth at bus and car.
A maxi-skirted girl strolls slowly by.
I turn and look. It might be you. But no.
Around me there's a 1970 sky.

Everywhere there are statues. Stone remains.
The mottled flesh is transient. On those trams,
invisible now but to the mind, you bore
your groceries home to the 1930 slums.
'There was such warmth,' you said. The gaslight hums
and large caped shadows tremble on the stair.
Now everything is brighter. Pale ghosts walk
among the spindly chairs, the birchen trees.
In lights of fiercer voltage you are less
visible than when in winter you
walked, a black figure, through the gaslight blue.

The past's an experience that we cannot share..
Flat-capped Glaswegians and the Music Hall.
Apples and oranges on an open stall.
A day in the country. And the sparkling Clyde
splashing its local sewage at the wall.
This April day shakes memories in a shade
opening and shutting like a parasol.
There is no site for the unshifting dead.
You're buried elsewhere though your flickering soul
is a constant tenant of my tenement.

You were happier here than anywhere, you said.
Such fine good neighbours helping when your child
almost died of croup. Those pleasant Wildes
removed with the fallen rubble have now gone
in the building programme which renews each stone.
I stand in a cleaner city, better fed,
in my diced coat, brown hat, my paler hands
leafing a copy of the latest book.
Dear ghosts, I love you, haunting sunlit winds,
dear happy dented ghosts, dear prodigal folk.

I left you, Glasgow, at the age of two
and so you are my birthplace just the same.
Divided city of the green and blue
I look for her in you, my constant aim
to find a ghost within a close who speaks
in Highland Gaelic.
                        The bulldozer breaks
raw bricks to powder. Boyish workmen hang
like sailors in tall rigging. Buildings sail
into the future. The old songs you sang
fade in their pop songs, scale on dizzying scale.

Iain Crichton Smith, 1970

George Square, c.1984 (George Oliver)

An Glaschu

Oidhche Shathuirn air Sràid Jamaica
is feasgar na Sàbaid air Great Western Road,
a' coiseachd 's a' coiseachd anns an t-saoghal ùr;
sìtheanan anns na gàrraidhean,
giobal 's an deoch air ann an doras bùthadh,
an Soisgeul a' tighinn rèidh ás a' chùbainn;
'Eil fada bho nach d'fhuair sibh bhon taigh?'

Is gaoth nan clobhsaichean,
is fasgadh ann an oisinn,
gaoth an iar-'eas le teanga fhliuch,
buntàta 's sgadan,
tiormachd na mine an cùl na h-amhach,
glagadaich ann an gàrradh nan soithichean,
a' chailleach a' gearain air prìs an èisg;
'Bi 'g òl ruma 's na bi sgrìobhadh dhachaigh.'

An daorach air Sràid Jamaica,
an traoghadh air Great Western Road,
an Soisgeul anns a' ghàrradh,
sìtheanan anns a' mhuilinn-fhlùir,
a' chailleach anns a' chlobhs,
is tiormachd ann an cùl na h-amhach;
'BHEIL FADA BHO NACH D'FHUAIR SIBH BHON TAIGH?'

In Glasgow

Saturday night on Jamaica Street
and Sunday evening on Great Western Road,
walking, walking in the new world;
flowers in the yards,
a young fellow, tight, in a shop doorway,
the Gospel coming quietly from the pulpit;
'Is it long since you heard from home?'

And the wind in the closes,
taking shelter in a corner,
a wet-tongued south-west wind,
potatoes and herring,
meal-dryness in the back of the throat,
a clatter in the shipyard,
the landlady complaining of the price of fish;
'Drink rum and don't write home.'

Jamaica Street plastered,
a dry throat on Great Western Road,
the Gospel in the Garden,
flowers in the meal-mill,
the old woman in the close,
and dryness at the back of the throat;
'IS IT LONG SINCE YOU HEARD FROM HOME?'

Ruaraidh MacThómais (Derick Thomson), 1970

In Glasgow

In my smoochy corner
take me on a cloud
I'll wrap you round
and lay you down
in smoky tinfoil
rings and records
sheets of whisky
and the moon all right
old pal all right
the moon all night

Mercy for the rainy
tyres and the violet
thunder that bring you
shambling and shy
from chains of Easterhouse

plains of lights
make your delight
in my nest my spell
my arms and my shell
my barn my bell

I've combed your hair
and washed your feet
and made you turn
like a dark eel
in my white bed
till morning lights
a silent cigarette
throw on your shirt
I lie staring yet
forget forget

Edwin Morgan, 1970

Nostalgie

Well, the George Squerr stchumers've pit the hems
oan Toonheid's answer tae London's Thames;
thuv peyed a squaad ooty Springburn broo
tae kinfront the Kinawl wi its Watterloo,
an dampt up Monklan's purlin stream
fur some dampt bailie's petrol dream,

some Tory nutter wi caurs oan the brain –
jis shows ye, canny leave nuthin alane,
the scunners.

Aye, thuv waistit Toonheid's claim tae fame,
an minny's the terrs Ah hud as a wean,
fishin fur roach aff the slevvery wa,
an pullin in luckies, mibbe a baw,
ur a bike, even, howked up ooty the glaur –
bit thuv timmed oot the watter, fur chuckies an taur,
jis cowped the Kinawl fulla slag, ten a penny,
an wheecht aw the luckies away tae the Clenny,
in hunners.

An thuv plankt the deid dugs aw swelt wi disease,
an pickt oot thur graves wi wee wizzent trees
tae relieve the monotony, eight tae a mile –
brek wan stick aff, thull gie ye the jile.
Ach, thurs nuthin tae beat a gude pie in the sky,
bit Ah've seen the Kinawl easy-oasyin by,
an it isnae the same Toonheid noo at aw,
an therrs even the rats is shootin the craw –
nae wunners.

Fur thuv drapped an Emm Wan oan the aul Toonheid,
an thurs nae merr dugs gonny float by deid –
jis caurs, jis breezin alang in the breeze,
terrin the leafs aff the hauf-bilet trees,
hell-bent fur the East (aye, yir no faur wrang),
wi thur taur an thur chuckies tae see thum alang –
ach, nivver mind, son, they kin aw go tae hell,
an we'll jis stick like the Monklan itsel –
non-runners.

Stephen Mulrine, 1971

207

Obituary

We two in W.2
walking,
and all the W.2 ladies, their
hair coiffed and corrugated come
with well-done faces
from the hairdressers.
We together
laughing,
in our snobbery of lovers,
at their narrow vowels
and strange permed poodles.
Locked too long in love, our eyes
were unaccustomed to the commonplace.
        Seems silly now really.

We two in W.2
walking
down Byres Road
passing unconcerned
a whole florist's
full of funerals,
the nightmare butcher's shop's
unnumbered horrors,
the hung fowls
and the cold fish
dead on the slab.
We saw ourselves duplicated
by the dozen in the chainstore
with no crisis of identity.
Headlines on newsagent's placards
caused us no alarm.
Sandwichman's prophecies of doom
just slid off our backs.
The television showroom's window

showed us cities burning
in black and white but we
had no flicker of interest.
An ambulance charged screaming past
but all we noticed was the funny old
Saturday street musician.
       Seems silly now really.

We two one Sunday
at the art galleries
looking only at each other.
We two one Sunday
in the museum –
wondering why the ownership of a famous man
should make a simple object a museum piece –
and I afraid
to tell you how
sometimes I did not wash your coffee cup for days
or touched the books you lent me
when I did not want to read.
Well, even at the time
       that seemed a bit silly really.

Christmas found me
with other fond and foolish girls
at the menswear counters
shopping for the ties that bind.
March found me
guilty of too much hope.
       Seems silly now really.

Liz Lochhead, 1971

A Dug A Dug

Hey, Daddy, wid ye get us a dug?
A big broon alsatian? Ur a wee white pug,
ur a skinny wee terrier ur a big fat bull?
Aw, Daddy! Get us a dug. Wull ye?

'n' whose dug'll it be when it messes the flerr?
'n' shites'n the carpet 'n' pees'n the sterr?
It's me ur yur mammy'll be taen fur a mug.
Away oot an' play. Yur no' needin' a dug.

Thomas Hay (George Oliver)

Bit, Daddy! Thur gien' thum away
doon therr at the RSPCA.
Yu'll get wan fur nothin' so ye wull.
Aw, Daddy. Get us a dug. Wull ye?

Doon therr at the RSPCA!
Dae ye hink Ah've goat nothin' else tae dae
bit get you a dug that Ah'll huftae mind?
Yur no' needin' a dug. Ye urny blind!

Bit, Daddy, it widnae be dear tae keep
'n' Ah'd make it a basket fur it tae sleep
'n' Ah'd take it fur runs away orr the hull.
Aw, Daddy. Get us a dug. Wull ye?

Dae ye hear 'im? Oan aboot dugs again?
Ah hink this yin's goat dugs 'n the brain.
Ah know whit ye'll get. A skite'n the lug
if Ah hear any merr aboot this bliddy dug.

Bit, Daddy, thur rerr fur guardin' the hoose
an' thur better'n cats fur catchin a moose
an' wee Danny's dug gies 'is barra a pull.
Aw, hey Daddy. Get us a dug. Wull ye?

Ah doan't hink thur's ever been emdy like you.
Ye could wheedle the twist oot a flamin' coarkscrew.
Noo get doon aff ma neck. Ah don't want a hug.
Awright. That's anuff. Ah'll get ye a dug.

Aw, Daddy! A dug! A dug!

William Keys, 1971

Glasgow Sonnets

i

A mean wind wanders through the backcourt trash.
Hackles on puddles rise, old mattresses
puff briefly and subside. Play-fortresses
of brick and bric-a-brac spill out some ash.
Four storeys have no windows left to smash,
but in the fifth a chipped sill buttresses
mother and daughter the last mistresses
of that black block condemned to stand, not crash.
Around them the cracks deepen, the rats crawl.
The kettle whimpers on a crazy hob.
Roses of mould grow from ceiling to wall.
The man lies late since he has lost his job,
smokes on one elbow, letting his coughs fall
thinly into an air too poor to rob.

ii

A shilpit dog fucks grimly by the close.
Late shadows lengthen slowly, slogans fade.
The YY PARTICK TOI grins from its shade
like the last strains of some lost *libera nos*
a malo. No deliverer ever rose
from these stone tombs to get the hell they made
unmade. The same weans never make the grade.
The same grey street sends back the ball it throws.
Under the darkness of a twisted pram
a cat's eyes glitter. Glittering stars press
between the silent chimney-cowls and cram
the higher spaces with their SOS.
Don't shine a torch on the ragwoman's dram.
Coats keep the evil cold out less and less.

iii

'See a tenement due for demolition?
I can get ye rooms in it, two, okay?
Seven hundred and nothin legal to pay
for it's no legal, see? That's my proposition,
ye can take it or leave it but. The position
is simple, you want a hoose, I say
for eight hundred pound it's yours.' And they,
trailing five bairns, accepted his omission
of the foul crumbling stairwell, windows wired
not glazed, the damp from the canal, the cooker
without pipes, packs of rats that never tired –
any more than the vandals bored with snooker
who stripped the neighbouring houses, howled, and fired
their aerosols – of squeaking 'Filthy lucre!'

iv

Down by the brickworks you get warm at least.
Surely soup-kitchens have gone out? It's not
the Thirties now. Hugh MacDiarmid forgot
in 'Glasgow 1960' that the feast
of reason and the flow of soul has ceased
to matter to the long unfinished plot
of heating frozen hands. We never got
an abstruse song that charmed the raging beast.
So you have nothing to lose but your chains,
dear Seventies. Dalmarnock, Maryhill,
Blackhill and Govan, better sticks and stanes
should break your banes, for poets' words are ill
to hurt ye. On the wrecker's ball the rains
of greeting cities drop and drink their fill.

v

'Let them eat cake' made no bones about it.
But we say let them eat the hope deferred

and that will sicken them. We have preferred
silent slipways to the riveters' wit.
And don't deny it – that's the ugly bit.
Ministers' tears might well have launched a herd
of bucking tankers if they'd been transferred
from Whitehall to the Clyde. And smiles don't fit
either. 'There'll be no bevvying' said Reid
at the work-in. But all the dignity you muster
can only give you back a mouth to feed
and rent to pay if what you lose in bluster
is no more than win patience with 'I need'
while distant blackboards use you as their duster.

vi

The North Sea oil-strike tilts east Scotland up,
and the great sick Clyde shivers in its bed.
But elegists can't hang themselves on fled-
from trees or poison a recycled cup –
If only a less faint, shaky sunup
glimmered through the skeletal shop and shed
and men washed round the piers like gold and spread
golder in soul than Mitsubishi or Krupp –
The images are ageless but the thing
is now. Without my images the men
ration their cigarettes, their children cling
to broken toys, their women wonder when
the doors will bang on laughter and a wing
over the firth be simply joy again.

vii

Environmentalists, ecologists
and conservationists are fine no doubt.
Pedestrianization will come out
fighting, riverside walks march off the lists,
pigeons and starlings be somnambulists
in far-off suburbs, the sandblaster's grout

multiply pink piebald façades to pout
at sticky-fingered mock-Venetianists.
Prop up's the motto. Splint the dying age.
Never displease the watchers from the grave.
Great when fake architecture was the rage,
but greater still to see what you can save.
The gutted double fake meets the adage:
a wig's the thing to beat both beard and shave.

viii

Meanwhile the flyovers breed loops of light
in curves that would have ravished tragic Toshy –
clean and unpompous, nothing wishy-washy.
Vistas swim out from the bulldozer's bite
by day, and banks of earthbound stars at night
begin. In Madame Emé's Sauchie Haugh, she
could never gain in leaves or larks or sploshy
lanes what's lost in a dead boarded site –
the life that overspill is overkill to.
Less is not more, and garden cities are
the flimsiest oxymoron to distil to.
And who wants to distil? Let bus and car
and hurrying umbrellas keep their skill to
feed ukiyo-e beyond Lochnagar.

ix

It groans and shakes, contracts and grows again.
Its giant broken shoulders shrug off rain.
It digs its pits to a shauchling refrain.
Roadworks and graveyards like their gallus men.
It fattens fires and murders in a pen
and lets them out in flaps and squalls of pain.
It sometimes tears its smoky counterpane
to hoist a bleary fist at nothing, then
at everything, you never know. The west
could still be laid with no one's tears like dust

and barricaded windows be the best
to see from till the shops, the ships, the trust
return like thunder. Give the Clyde the rest.
Man and the sea make cities as they must.

x

From thirtieth-floor windows at Red Road
he can see choughs and samphires, dreadful trade –
the schoolboy reading *Lear* has that scene made.
A multi is a sonnet stretched to ode
and some say that's no joke. The gentle load
of souls in clouds, vertiginously stayed
above the windy courts, is probed and weighed.
Each monolith stands patient, ah'd and oh'd.
And stalled lifts generating high-rise blues
can be set loose. But stalled lives never budge.
They linger in the single-ends that use
their spirit to the bone, and when they trudge
from closemouth to laundrette their steady shoes
carry a world that weighs us like a judge.

Edwin Morgan, 1972

Lament for a Lost Dinner Ticket

See ma mammy
See ma dinner ticket
A pititnma
Pokit an she pititny
Washnmachine.

See thon burnty
Up wherra firewiz

Ma mammy says Am no tellnyagain
No'y playnit.
A jist wen'y eatma
Pokacrisps furma dinner
Nabigwoffldoon.

The wummin sed Aver near
Clapsd
Jistur heednur
Wee wellies sticknoot.

They sed Wot heppind?
Nme'nma belly
Na bedna hospital.
A sed A pititnma
Pokit an she pititny
Washnmachine.

They sed Ees thees chaild eb slootly
Non verbal?
A sed MA BUMSAIR
Nwen'y sleep.

Margaret Hamilton, 1972

Something I'm Not

familiar with, the tune
of their talking, comes tumbling before them
down the stairs which (oh I forgot) it was my turn
to do again this week.
My neighbour and my neighbour's child. I nod, we're not
on speaking terms exactly.

I don't know much about her. Her dinners smell
different. Her husband's a busdriver,
so I believe.
She carries home her groceries in Grandfare bags
though I've seen her once or twice around the corner
at Shastri's for spices and such.
(I always shop there – he's open till all hours
making good). How does she feel?
Her children grow up with foreign accents,
swearing in fluent Glaswegian. Her face
is sullen. Her coat is drab plaid, hides
but for a hint at the hem, her sari's
gold embroidered gorgeousness. She has
a jewel in her nostril.
The golden hands with the almond nails
that push the pram turn blue
in this city's cold climate.

Liz Lochhead, 1972

Carnival

Glass roof holds down a
stale air of excitement,
bottles up noise.
It's all screams and legs
cutting prescribed arcs. We walk.
The lights revolve around you.
People spin at tangents,
swing limit-wards on chain end.
Collisions are less than inevitable.

The speedway is a whirlpool.
The waltzer reels out-of-time

to ten popsongs.
Pressures force skirts up. Girls bare
their teeth and scream.
You say it's screams of pleasure.
The timid roll pennies.

Aunt Sally has ten men. They
grin and shake their heads. I
miss the point.
The hall of mirrors hints at all sorts
of horrible distortions, but
you're favourably reflected in my eyes.
We play the fruit machines.

I spin to a mere blur on a wheelspoke
about your axis. There is a smell of onions
and axle grease.
The ghost train has pop-up fears for fun,
makes me laugh off mine and try
octopus, big dipper, roller coaster.
(Single riders pay double fare.)

Here is no plain sailing, all bump
and jerk. Above the screams, the sound
of some clown laughing.
Showmen shuffle hoops, push darts.
Prizes are sheer trash, and every lady wins.
You buy me candy floss and smile.
I sink my teeth into sweet damn all.

Liz Lochhead, 1972

from A Sense of Order

Sunday Walk
I stop at the foot of Garioch Drive
Where my aunt used to live
Three floors up.
                    I remember the smell
Of camomile that hit you in the hall,
The embroidered sampler, the jars
Of wax chrysanths, the budgerigars
In their lacquered cage; the ladies who came
To read the Bible in the front room –
Surrounded by marzipan, and dragons
On silky screens.
                    A rag-and-bone man,
His pony ready for the knacker's yard,
Rounds a corner (short of a tail-light)
And disappears up Clouston Street.

Below, the Kelvin runs like stinking lard.

Period Piece
Hand in hand, the girls glide
Along Great Western Road.
                              Outside
The Silver Slipper the boys wait,
Trousers flared, jacket-pockets
Bulging with carry-outs.
The girls approach. A redhead pouts,
Sticks her tongue out,
Then passes under the strung lights
To the dance-floor. 'I'll have it
Off with that one.' 'Want to bet?'
'I'd rather lumber her mate . . .'

They nick their cigarettes.
                              Inside,
The miniskirts are on parade,
Listening to The Marmalade.

Stewart Conn, 1972

Family Visit

Laying linoleum, my father spends hours
With his tape measure,
Littering the floor
As he checks his figures, gets
The angle right; then cuts
Carefully, to the music
Of a slow logic. In despair
I conjure up a room where
A boy sits and plays with coloured bricks.

My mind tugging at its traces,
I see him in more dapper days
Outside the Kibble Palace
With my grandfather, having
His snapshot taken; men firing
That year's leaves.
The Gardens are only a stone's throw
From where I live . . . But now
A younger self comes clutching at my sleeve.

Or off to Innellan, singing, we would go,
Boarding the steamer at the Broomielaw
In broad summer, these boomps-a-daisy
Days, the ship's band playing in a lazy

Botanic Gardens, 1938 (Ian Fleming)

Swell, my father steering well clear
Of the bar, mother making neat
Packets of waste-paper to carry
To the nearest basket or (more likely)
All the way back to Cranworth Street.

Leaving my father at it
(He'd rather be alone) I take
My mother through the changed Botanics.
The bandstand is gone, and the great
Rain-barrels that used to rot
And overflow. Everything is neat
And plastic. And it is I who must walk
Slowly for her, past the sludge
And pocked marble of Queen Margaret Bridge.

Stewart Conn, 1972

Seen Out

Over small print in papers,
arguments at Public Inquiries,
a demolition squad moves in;
coloured helmets swarming up to
patched roofs, unpicking rafters,
levering slabs through ceilings,
gulping cupboards sheer with air.
Now and then a tenement
fights back, stumps snarling
chokes of dust, menacing
what once had been a passing street.
Machines bring all stone
down to its own level.

On a half-cleared site where soon
rows of red and yellow curtains
would be switched-on stacks of lights,
I found the handle of a pan,
a mattress spring, a chair's leg,
the bric-a-brac of done-with caring;
while from one grey isolated
tenement storey, with cushions,
blandishments and blankets
they prised loose an old woman
from a sense of place that hadn't
quite seen out her time.

Maurice Lindsay, 1973

The Girl I Met in Byres Road

At night I can't remember her, or ever unwounded
With a happy face. We came together too often
With knives in our hands for happiness to
Come out of the struggle.

        I often said
I'd leave her, and she left me, often enough.
We never talked together: long conflicting monologues
Took place between us.

        That was Glasgow
When we were young. You don't have good memories
Of something like that.

        So let me say this
About her: if we went our own ways, and never
Properly parted, it was because we never properly
Met. Two other shadows joined in the darkness
And the shadows that were ourselves remained
Alone.

Robin Hamilton, 1973

'there was that time charlie tully'

there was that time charlie tully
took a corner kick
an' you know how he

wus always great at gettin thaem
tae curve in, well charlie takes the corner
and it curved in and fuck me did the wind
no cerry it right intae the net. but they
disputed it. and the linesman hud the
flag up and they goat away wae it and tully
hud tae take it again. an' fuck me does he no get
it in the net again. you should've
seen it. it just seemed tae go roon
in a kind o' hauf curcle. above aw their
heids. fuckin' keeper didnae know where tae look.
and there was that time john cassidy went into
the toilet and there was no
lightbulb and he just had to fix up with some
water he found in a bucket. and here it was piss.
he didnae discover it until it was actually in
him. he was very sick after that. he goat
very bad jaundice.

Tom McGrath, 1973

On John Maclean

'I am not prepared to let Moscow dictate to Glasgow.'
Failures may be interesting, but it is the firmness
of what he wanted and did not want
that raises eyebrows: when does the quixotic
begin to gel, begin to impress, at what point
of naked surprise?
            'I for one will not follow
a policy dictated by Lenin until he knows
the situation more clearly.'
                    Which Lenin hadn't time to,
and parties never did – the rock of nations

like the rock of ages, saw-toothed, half-submerged,
a cranky sputtering lighthouse somewhere, as often
out as lit, a wreck of ships all round,
there's the old barnacled 'Workingclass Solidarity',
and 'International Brotherhood' ripped open and awash,
while you can see the sleekit 'Great-Power Chauvinism'
steaming cannily past on the horizon
as if she had never heard of *cuius regio*.
Maclean wanted neither the maimed ships
nor the paradox of not wanting them
while he painfully trimmed the lighthouse lamp
to let them know that Scotland was not Britain
and writs of captains on the Thames
would never run in grey Clyde waters.

Well, nothing's permanent. It's true he lost –
a voice silenced in November fog. Party
is where he failed, for he believed in people,
not in *partiinost'* that as everyone knows
delivers the goods. Does it? Of course.
And if they're damaged in transit you make do?
You do – and don't be so naive about this world!
Maclean was not naive, but
                'We are out
for life and all that life can give us'

was what he said, that's what he said.

Edwin Morgan, 1973

(George Oliver)

By the Preaching of the Word

let gallows languish
let gas flurry
let glowworms fetch
let galluses flash
let geggies launch
let galoshes fish
let gasteropods munch
let gashes flinch
let glass vanish
let gases flush
let gaggles nourish
let goggles crunch
let Gagool fumble
let assegais frolic
let cargoes lurch
let Owlglass shuffle
let laughter urge
let lassies fudge
let lashes fash
let laggards finish
let Gardners furnish
let glasses varnish
let Gogol lunch
let grasses worry

let gags fashion
let sago munch
let gorgeous tundish
let garages burnish
let gorges brandish
let gargoyles forage
let gaffers ravage
let gavels hurry
let gravel crush
let gunwales crash
let grannies touch
let gurges famish
let gambols clinch
let gutters rush
let galaxies usher
let starfish grumble
let fungus gush
let gasmen gamble
let lurchers shamble
let gundogs fadge
let gasbags fuddle
let flunkeys gargle
let flags garnish
let Brasso furbish
LET GLASGOW FLOURISH

Edwin Morgan, 1974

227

Pigeons in George Square

Pigeons, pee-gulls,
urchins' equals,
civic defecators,
public decorators,
deacons, dowagers,
skarters, scavengers,
earth-boats, roof-ducks,
doxies for noon drunks,
puffed up anyhow:
citizens of Glasgow.

Anne Stevenson, 1974

Tea Time

ahm thaht depehhhhndint
hingoanti ma vowwwwulz
hingoanti ma maaaammi

howz thi time

ma manz thaht diffffrint
awfa shoart vowwwwulz
hizthaht indipehhhhndint

ahl bettr away

Tom Leonard, 1975

To Lesbia's Husband

Gaun ye clown
ye canny see
through Lesbia furiver
cursin me

Roar an laff

it's nothin new
thit you'd be better aff
if she effed at you.

Catullus (83), translated by David Neilson, 1975

Gorbals

Spence and Matthew manufactured
Concrete cliffs shape the new Gorbals.
But the old culture survives on odd brick fragments
Liberated into sight by the aerosol.
CUMBIES, TONGS and TOIS
Record their war cries
In strangely elegant graffiti
With the spiderspun delicacy
Of a Steinberg drawing.

A fine tall looping 'C'
A fat short 'U' and the other letters
Mark that the CUMBIES passed this way.

Other factions intertwine and overcross
In a lacework of white on rusty brick
Against the grey of the carefully calculated new tenements.

But this is all accident,
Part of this accidental city.

Tom Berry, 1977

The Bargain

The river in January is fast and high.
You and I
are off to the Barrows.
Gathering police-horses twitch and fret
at the Tron end of London Road and Gallowgate.
The early kick-off we forgot
has us three-thirty rubbing the wrong way
against all the ugly losers
getting ready to let fly
where the two rivers meet.

January
and we're looking back   looking forward
don't know which way.

But the boy with the three
beautiful bakelite
Bush radios for sale in Meadow's minimarket is
buttonpopping stationhopping he
doesn't miss a beat   sings along   it's easy
to every changing tune.

Yes today we're in love aren't we?
with the whole splintering city
its big quick river   wintry bridges
its brazen black Victorian heart.
So what if every other tenement
wears its hearth on its gable end
all I want
is my glad eye to catch
a glint in your flinty Northern face again
just once.   Oh I know it's cold
and coming down
and no we never lingered long among the Shipbank traders.
Paddy's Market   underneath the arches
stank too much today –
the usual wetdog reek
rising from piles of old damp clothes.
Somebody absolutely steamboats he says on sweet warm wine
swigged plaincover from a paperbag
squats in a puddle with nothing to sell
but three bent forks   a torn
calendar (last year's)
and a single broken plastic sandal.
So we hadn't the stomach for it today.
Oh you could say
we don't deserve a bargain then.
No connoisseur can afford to be too scrupulous
about keeping his hands clean.
There was no doubt   the rare   the beautiful
and the bugle-beaded   the real antique   dirt cheap
among the rags and drunks
you could easily take to the cleaners.

At the Barrows though everything has its price
no haggling   believe me
this boy knows his radios.
Pure Utility
and what that's worth these days.
Suddenly the Fifties are fashionable
and anything within a decade of art deco
a rarity you'll pay through the nose for.

The man with the patter and all these curtain lengths
in fibreglass is flabbergasted at the bargain
and says so in so many words.
Jesus every other
arcade around here's
a Fire Surround Boutique. –

We watch one struggling family
father carrying hearth home
mother wound up with kids.
All the couples we know
fall apart or have kids.
Oh we've never shouldered much
we'll stick to small ikons
(as long as they're portable) for our home –
a dartboard   a peacock feather
a stucco photoframe.

We queue in the blue
blue haze of hot fat
for Danny's Do-nuts that grit
our teeth with granulated sugar.
I lose you and find you
lose you again.
Now two stalls away you thumb
through a complete set of manuals for primary teachers from
the nineteen-thirties.
I rub my sleeve
on a dusty Chinese saucer
till the gilt shows through.
Oh come on   we promised
we'd not let our affection for the slightly cracked
trap us into such expenditure again.
Oh even if it is a bargain
we won't buy.
The stallholder says we'll be the death of her.
She says   see January
it's been the doldrums the day.

And it's packing up time
with the dark coming early
and as cold as the river.
At the bus-stop I show you
the beady bag and the maybe rosewood box
with the inlaid butterfly and the broken catch.
You've bought
a record by the Shangri-Las
a pinstripe waistcoat that needs a stitch
it just won't get   and a book called 'Enquire
Within – Upon Everything'.
The raw cold gets colder.
There doesn't seem to be a lot to say.
I wish we could either mend things
or learn to throw them away.

Liz Lochhead, 1977

Ghosts

My face against the bars
of your cot, close to yours,

I listen while you whisper
urgently, telling me where

you want to go. Needless
to say, it is the Kibble Palace.

As soon as you are dressed
and have had breakfast

we set off; a fine
mist rising from the Kelvin.

We are alone in the Gardens.
Leaving the pram at the entrance

I take you to where the goldfish are.
For what seems hours, you peer

through the murky
water. Under the lattice-work

of white spars, whose
curved glass has

mirrored family upon family,
we too shall soon be,

like my father and grandfather,
ghosts in the empty air.

Stewart Conn, 1978

233

Glasgow

I have just finished reading MacDiarmid's poem
On the fair city of Glasgow
And to tell the truth I never recognised a single thing
Not one word sprang up from the pages
To remind me of a single place I had visited
Or recalled to mind the essential character of the city
He says it's the houses that make Glasgow not the people
Well houses are not a permanent feature of any city
The whole character of a place can change in a hundred years
But the one thing that doesn't change is the people
The people who live in it every day of their life
Travelling to work and generally keep the city going
If I had to write a poem on the city of Glasgow
I would mention first of all the pubs
And the betting shops
O yes there's more pubs and betting shops in Glasgow
Per head of population
Than in any city in the country
This doesn't say much for our reputation abroad
But when you come to the city I guarantee
You'll never have a dull moment
Not if you're a drinking man
And like a wee flutter on the gee-gees
Which is how maist o the people in this toon
Tend to spend their time
Which in no way reflects on the city
But on the contrary gies to the citizens
The certain spark and spriteliness of step
That you meet on every coarner
Wi the wee Glesca keelie as how we natives are called
Busily running roond spending his last few coppers
Fur Glesca people are no great savers
It's completely contrary to their whole way of life
And wud be disaster to the economic structure of the city

To say nothing of the revolution it would cause in banking circles
Which is another peculiarity of the city that strikes me
You know the wee man that stauns at the coarner
Wi the wee stump o a fag-end
Hingin from his mooth
And just the beginning of a slight hump
Not a pretty picture but it's there aw the same
Croonin away to his chinas in what must seem like a foreign language
To anybody who happens to hear it
Imagine Glesca folk walking aboot
Wi bank books up their jooks
A wid be feart tae be seen in the street wi wan
In case it fell oot
Whit an embarrassment
The only book A carry about is the old battered rent book
And even then when A'm no in arrears
It's a long time since it seen the light o day
A think it would disintegrate if A laid a finger on it
So much for boozin and speculative enterprise
On the four-legged stock exchange
Another thing A like is these new drinking laws
They're about to introduce especially
Drinking on a Sunday
That's what I call progress
I don't seem to be able to get off the subject of drink
Still I've got a soft spot for it
But do you remember when you were at school
And you used to play about on the back dykes
Challenging your friends to see who could jump the furthest
Or who was most daring in thinking up new things to do
And when the middens were always on fire
But that was when they had coal fires
None of yir smokeless rubbish
Or two big iron bars staring at you from the walls
The coal fires were great
You could throw anything on them
And whit a welcome they gied ye when ye come in from the cauld
Ye goat a haud i the big poker
That was ay lyin at the side
And stoked it up till ye had a big blazer gawn

And that was you till it was somebody else's turn
Tae fetch mer coal in from the bunker outside
Ye were really posh if ye had a bunker inside
Or on the landin
But A really hated when ye had to go ootside
In the freezing cauld
And fill up a daft pail
And hid tae start brekin up those big lumps
Wi a stupid hammer
It was really idiotic but it hid tae be done
If ye were really fly ye kept a coupla big pails
Filled in the loaby and whit ye didny drap
On the flerboards ye flung on the fire
Straight from the bucket
Then ye sat back and watched the flames
Licking the ceiling
Aw the different colours aw mixed up
The blues the greens and purples
That wis as cosy as ye were ever likely tae get
Aw fur the cost of a few daft pennies
That ye stuck in the meter
That wis when ye found oot who yir real friends really were
When the light suddenly went oot
And yis are aw sittin there in the dark
Waitin to see who's gonny make a move
Listenin fur the sound of money
And gropin yir way in the dark
Feelin the furniture
Aw it wis nae joke
But ye hid a laugh
If ye didny ye went spare
And started dreamin aw soarts o things
And people thought ye were gone balmy
But maist people didny care anyway
They hid their ain things tae think aboot
An wirny worried aboot you
They just let ye get oan wi it
That was whit A liked maist naebody bothered ye
If you didny bother them
Another thing A liked

Wis that when ye wirny feeling too weel
There wis always some cheery soul
Tae brighten up yir day
And make ye feel things wurny as bad as they seem
So it's no such a bad place in the end
And A'm glad A've been able tae putt doon on paper
A few a its good points
At the same time no glossin err the fact
That when looked at from the ootside
It seems nae different fae anywhere else
Perhaps it aw depends where yir staunin
And whose shoes yir wearin at the time
But anyway A'm no sorry fur breakin intae Glesca slang
And if A broaght back a few memories fur anybody
Well it's no exactly been a waste o time
A know there's hunners o things A should have mentioned
But ye canny think o everything at wance.

William Gilfedder, 1979

Glasgow 1956

There's always a headscarf stooped
into a pram, nodding in time
with a plastic rattle, outside a shop
advertising a sale of wallpaper.

There's a queue facing another queue
like chessmen across the street;
a hearse standing at a petrol-pump
as the chauffeur tests the tyres,

Crosshill, 1976 (George Oliver)

the undertaker brushes ash off
his morning paper, and my mother,

looking down at me looking up,
is telling me not to point.

The background is a level site
where we recreate the war.
Calder Street is Calder Street,
level as far as the Clyde.

Without a tree to denote it,
the season is moot. That faint
thunder is the Cathcart tram,
and the sky is white as a trousseau

posed against blackened bricks.
A grey posy in her hands,
the bride stands smiling there
for decades, waiting for the click.

Gerald Mangan, 1980

Jingle

This is the bell that never rang

This
RANG
This is
RANG RANG
This is the bell
RANG
This is the bell that
RANG
This is never
RANG

This is never the bell that
RANG
This is the rang bell
RANG RANG RANG
This is the bell that
RANG RANG RANG RANG
                            never

This is the tree that never grew

This tree never grew green
This green tree never grew
Neverever green grew this tree
This tree grew never evergreen

This is the bird that never flew

this is the
            bird
this is the
            bird
this wee
            bird
teenie
            bird
totie
            bird
chookie
            bird
this is the
            bird
it never
            flew
never
            flew
never
            flew
never
            flew
aw!

This is the fish that never swam

this is the fish
tell me who I am
fish out of water
never ever swam

Alan Spence, 1981

Sometimes it's Hard to be a Woman

Sometimes it's hard to be a woman
Giving all your love to jist wan Man –
You'll have bad times
He'll have good times
Goin' oot on the randan
But if you love him
You'll forgive him
Bite your tongue and pass another can
And if you love him
Be proud of him
'Cause after all he's Jist a Man.

Stand by your Man
Send oot fur pudding suppers –
When you are on your uppers,
Eat spam yoursel', buy pope'seye
Tae feed your Man –
A decent wummin aye hus
Some squerr-slice in her frying pan
To satisfy her Man.

Sometimes it's hard to be a woman
Stuck in wi' the weans without your Man –

Though he gets pished on peyday
Never mind hen, every Friday
He'll bring you hame a Babycham
If he tends to thump ye
Before he tries to hump ye
Then snores while you lie hatching up a plan
To up and leave the schunner
Oh is it ony wunner
If you can't bloody stand your Man.

Liz Lochhead, 1982

Clydegrad

It was so fine we lingered there for hours.
The long broad streets shone strongly after rain.
Sunset blinded the tremble of the crane
we watched from, dazed the heliport-towers.
The mile-high buildings flashed, flushed, greyed, went dark,
greyed, flushed, flashed, chameleons under flak
of cloud and sun. The last far thunder-sack
ripped and spilled its grumble. Ziggurat-stark,
a power-house reflected in the lead
of the old twilight river leapt alive
lit up at every window, and a boat
of students rowed past, slid from black to red
into the blaze. But where will they arrive
with all, boat, city, earth, like them, afloat?

Edwin Morgan, 1983

Matt McGinn

We cannot see it, it keeps changing so.
All round us, *in and out, above, below,*
at evening, *phantom figures come and go,*
silently, *just a magic shadow show.*
A hoarse voice singing *come love watch with me*
was all we heard on that fog-shrouded bank.
We thought we saw him, but if so, he sank
into the irrecoverable sea.
Dear merry man, what is your country now?
Does it keep changing? Will we ever see it?
A crane, a backcourt, an accordion?
Or sherbet dabs, henna, and jasmined brow?
The book is clasped, and time will never free it.
Mektub. The caravan winds jangling on.

Edwin Morgan, 1983

Parachuting into Glasgow

(for Steve and Sue)

Be born
From the throbbing fuselage, out
Through laundromat-spill at the round door
Under the hull in sudsy cloud birling
Upwards, weathermap that plummets
Upwards and round. The roulette wheel of
Bishopbriggs, Gilbertfield, Blairdardie, Campsies
That cry at emerging with the ripped cord

Into holdable slowness, unaffordable, slapped, gifted
On a plate brimmed with uplands, moored
To the Clyde's rich split. Hover, protean. Glide into
A boy with a bouzouki in an archway strumming
Light from pavingstones pink beneath warm
Martini umbrellas. A bronze statue. Float
Over shoppers' heads. Heat and brightness, white bread
Tucked in a basket, spread the pizzicato
Wine whine of laughter, capped
With white coins. In the pedestrian precinct buy
A handbook to dancing, an underskirt, a TV
With your eyes only; recharge
Over benches and borders. Ease your shoe off. Ogle. Pinch yourself
And be melted down, re-formed, re-set
As the woman made of carrots, the chuckler,
The liquid Buchanan Street, its bouzouki. On touchdown
Stay various: the lost phone number
Dropped in the street; cackle; the nameless
Passers by – be them; assume
A shopping trolley, a red waistcoat, a cloudless evening sky.
It is Thursday. Coo like a pigeon. Eat. Like St Mungo
Mark this place with a cross.

Robert Crawford, 1984

A Glasgow Cassandra

(Ode 'A Cassandre')

Sweetheart, here's a rose, wid ye look
That jist this mornin sashayed oot
In a new rid froack tae greet the dawn;
Noo see if it's no, at the endy the day,
Right oot the gemme, an certainly no way
A match fur you, sweetheart, come on –

See, look, in jist a coupla hours
It's jined the ranks a faded flowers,
A scarlet wumman turned pale pink;
It's tough, bit that's the wey it goes,
Premier League, an nixt – deid rose –
A damn sight quicker than ye'd think.

So get the message, sweetheart, eh?
Gether rosebuds while ye may,
While the goin's good, move fast;
Get wired in, yir auntie's blind,
An keep this rose aye in yir mind,
Fur wan thing's sure, it disnae last.

Ronsard, *translated by Stephen Mulrine*, 1985

Gunfight at the Govan Corral

Leather-skinned from the desert heat,
Jingling spurs on stirruped feet,
A stranger rides down Calder Street.

Weathered stetson pulled down low,
He's six days' ride from Mexico.
The tram-lines make the going slow.

Tall and gaunt and saddle-weary,
Caked in dust from the endless prairie,
He's got his sights on Gordon Carey –

The rattlesnake from Gorbals Cross,
Who stole his sweetheart, Senga Ross.
If he bites the dust, it's no one's loss.

From the high sierras of Maryhill,
Through tumbleweed in Provanmill,
He's trailed him; now he'll shoot to kill.

Colt Forty-Fives slung low on his hips,
A smoking lolly between his lips,
He's reining up for a bag of chips.

Blue eyes crinkled against the glare,
He's tethering his thirsty mare
When a gunshot shatters the brooding air.

Dust spurts up, beside his boot:
Carey's missed him by a foot.
He dives for the Co-op door, and shoots.

Come out, he yells, *and show some pride,*
You yellow skunk. You stole the bride
of the fastest gun in Kelvinside.

Facing his doom with tight-set jaws,
As the clock strikes, and a buzzard caws,
The villain snarls a curse, and draws.

A blink of the eye is all it takes
To miss the move the stranger makes.
Slick and smooth as the tongue of a snake,

His muzzle spits a deadly flame.
The bullet bearing Carey's name
Finds its mark, and ends his game.

The hero blows his nails, and strolls
Home for his tea. The credits roll.
The sun sets over the Govan Toll.

Gerald Mangan, 1986

'You have returned to Glasgow after a long exile'

You have returned to Glasgow after a long exile.
A *Glasgow Herald* special edition is selling like hot cakes.
It publishes a Turkish poet's abstruse new song.

This Turkish poet is of an international cast of mind.
He also has an unselfconscious enjoyment of working-class culture.
In fact, his song is about a match between Glasgow Celtic and Glasgow
   Rangers.

A certain Professor MacFadyen has detected the influence of MacDiarmid.

Tom Leonard, 1986

James Maxton

Made by the Clyde and unmade by the Thames,
His words were mair volcanic nor his deeds.
We honour his passion, honour his noble aims
Mair nor aucht he achieved for Scotland's needs.
Mithered by Glescae, frae her iron dugs
He sucked his love o the sufferan human race:
Grieved owre the scabbit bairn in its bed o bugs,
And kendlet his ire at ilka stairvan face.

Born o a man-made wasterie o stane,
He wrocht to make yon desart burgeon green,

Gar new sang braird frae its mirk hert o pain;
And his vision-torkit mind and hauntit een
Clawcht sicht o, throu ilk beelan Glescae slum,
The lineaments o New Jerusalem.

Tom Scott, 1987

Plain Speaking

I put it to you plainly, as when
in your dark blouse you bend
by the couch where I am writing
to kiss me goodnight, as you lean

forward a little to read these
words – clear as the sheen on new-turned
clay tonight by the garden fence
where the streetlamp burns

or sheer as the Clyde at midnight sketching
plans for a city where no one talks
while cargoes to tease or break the mind
float by in a sodden box.

Now lighted windows blink: folk fold up
today. Most of the people I've known
turning to sleep. Like old cats
hearts ease into the dark alone

and, plainly I tell you, it welcomes them home.

James McGonigal, 1987

Birds of Passage

Up on Partickhill
from the space where a house has been
you can eyeball the cranes
and the frosted meniscus
of the gasometer,
and read the high flats
like bar charts across the city.

Backs to the Atlantic
the foolish cranes
drooling chains and hooks
stare in rigid unison
up the shipless river.

The weathercock on the steeple
abandoned by last week's westerly
cannot avert his metallic eye,
gazing down the lower reaches
of the vacant estuary.

Across the twilight
a swarm of starlings
draws its skein,
dancing a dotted veil
over their rusting kin.

Valerie Thornton, 1987

Kelvinbridge: A Node

1.

A terrible day – strong winds, heavy rain. After reading
from books by Russians for most of the morning, I decide
to go for my dinner to the Chinese restaurant
two bridges away – two bridges over
the same winding river. That should take me
some way towards the centre of town, as it is.
To my surprise, people are already there,
though the place opened only 20 minutes before, and they
are towards the end of their meals. Quietly,
I manoeuvre my spoon through a bowl of thick soup,
until only the sight of the wet window reminds me
of the foul weather outside. Behind me,
a man and a woman begin to talk loudly
to the restaurateur. They are preparing to leave.
They are now going to the sauna baths in Paisley.
Paisley! The very word speaks of failed driving tests,
and Americans working in the Technical College.
I gaze down at that city from the train
when I go to visit my parents, and, again,
in much the same way, when I return. More discussion
follows – and it was in 1920
(the man offers), which was a long time ago;
in 1920, which was a very long time ago,
that my elder brother, in Elmbank Street –.
No, I remember: first he said that, long ago,
he had an aunt whom he used to visit, who lived
in Park Road, which is just round the corner from here.
Indeed it is – it is 15 seconds' walk away.
And it was in 1920, which is a long time ago now,
that my elder brother, at the corner of
Elmbank Street – no, not Elmbank Street – what is it called? –
at the corner of Woodlands Road and Park Road –
he was killed. He was knocked over by a lorry

which mounted the pavement. He was 6. Six,
asked the restaurant owner, having to say something.
Six. Yes. It's a long time ago now.
(I'm sure my own mother was born the following year.)
We may be certain this was not a Chinese
restaurant then. But, whatever it was,
some discussion of the local fatality
was surely carried on here, here, in this actual space,
in the broad area of this disappearing bowl of soup,
65 years ago. (Ah, while I remember, the poet
Philip Larkin, died in hospital yesterday,
at the age of 63.) And off they go
to their sauna in Paisley, their comfort thrice a week:
on Tuesday, on Thursday, and on Saturday.
Soon after, over a cup of charmless tea,
I am reading a few more pages about Mandelshtam.
About how once he bought a volume of Kant,
(circa 1930, I suppose), glanced through it, sniffed,
said, 'Nadia, this isn't for us,' and tossed the object
behind a pile of other books, out of harm's way.
Then I went out again, into the unstopping rain,
and, 15 seconds later, turned into Park Road,
opposite a shop where, in my own childhood,
I bought, in ones and twos, whole herds of model animals,
and, two minutes later, turned out of Park Road again
at the corner of Elmbank Street – No, sorry, Woodlands Road.
A few cars were hurrying past, as usual.

2.
fortunately the dead
cannot all laugh at once
however hard they try

3.
I am walking home, tentatively, after seeing
a play about nuclear extinction, (and the full moon
looks even less credible than ever), past
a row of shops near a bridge, which contain
a small still-open store where I buy a packet
of biscuits (it is now several days

since I finished them), and a still-lit place
of a certain dubiousness, which seems to be
a massage-parlour, or some such exotic location,
wherein, who can tell what strange impending convulsions –
when a child on a bicycle collided with me.
I cannot remember if, at that moment,
I was still trying to console myself with the thought
that, well, it all presumably must end
('it' being life etcetera – I would prefer
not to define the 'etcetera' – not at the moment,
anyway), it presumably all must end
at some time or another, and perhaps
something gothic and colossal in the sky
could strike the earth at any moment, and that
would be that ('that' being, presumably,
a considerable amount of small new planets).
Even if it was so, it would not sound plausible.
I stopped her from falling, and she stopped the cycle from falling,
and what keeps the earth from falling I do not know.
Then, after a brief exchange of enquiries
about the other's health – repeated on my side,
not so on hers – she cycled onwards again,
across the bridge, with noticeably inadequate
technique, slowing and stopping awkwardly
at the other side, and dragging the bike round
onto a return journey. When she reached me,
coming back, she in no way acknowledged me –
that is, beyond paying me the compliment
of careful avoidance. So she went past.
And I am sure of this, that even by the time she had turned,
it had struck me as somehow being unimaginable
that a planet which contained such a complex creature
could possibly be destroyed. However,
instead of hitting me, she could have skidded off
the pavement entirely, onto the noisy road,
and the first thing I knew of her could have been
a sound of metal buckling nearby. This proves nothing.
Even less than did the momentary grasping
of her left elbow, in my hand. Will she have children,
I wonder, and, if so, will there still be bicycles,

and irrelevant self-absorbed theatregoers, to run into
in a sky still unclear with flying projectiles?
And, if not, where will the point of convergence lie?
And if we all survive for a hundred years,
who will be crossing this bridge, and for what reason,
and what, may I ask, will have just collided with what?

Frank Kuppner, 1988

Inner Glasgow

You were a small red coat among the pit bings
That aren't there now, between Cambuslang
And Shettleston, with *Tell Me Why, Look and Learn*;

The quays have altered, liners replaced by jasmine;
Where docks are cultivated, hard nostalgia
Steam-rivets us to ghosts we love, in murals

Where everybody looks the same and sings
Of oppression, smokes, drinks lager, shouts out 'fuck'.
Shops sell us. Entrepreneurs' industrial

Museums postcard grime; we're pseudo-Griersonned.
But you refuse these foisted images, stay
Too true, still here, grown up in your red coat.

My inner Glasgow, you don't leave me, I
Do not leave you. A tubular steel frontage, roadcones
Flash towards us like the tiny folded pictures

In pop-up books, the lovely, lovely details
Too close to label art, that bring on laughter
When words cut out their starter motor, leaving us

Idling beside a cloudless firth. Those shorelights
Spread beyond Millport, beckon us to marry,
To lie along the bowsprits of our lives.

Robert Crawford, 1988

Joan Eardley

The sea is a wall.
There is no latticework of air among the waves,
Only tenemented stone
Rigid with the desire to breathe.

Children's faces poke from it,
Shadowed pebbles, flakes
Of slate chips chattering in the sea.

One thinks she has seen a beautiful shell
In Tillie street:
A small boy lifts up
Triumphant broken glass.

The wall is a sea.
Its waves pretend a light and midnight breeze
That breathe of their desire
To build children from its crumbling shell.

David Kinloch, 1989

Carbolic Dan

Dan McKinnon,
a Lochboisdale man,
sailed the blue world from the Broomielaw.
A laughing man,
all walrus moustache and beery breath
to nephews. 'A kiss for you, my little man.'
The black shoes patent leather
and the socks bright blue;
the shoulders like a bottle's neck.
To fellow Gaels he was Dan Ban
but the keelies called him for a slip
in a language not his own.
'This new hydraulic cran's
the coming thing,' they let him know,
and 'Aye,' he would repeat, for show,
'A great thing, this carbolic cran.'
In my father's thoughts
his uncle rolls along the Paisley Road:
Carbolic Dan.

Michael Munro, 1989

The Journeyman

Wurkin piecewurk in the funnel shoap,
buildin quick
but no quick enough,
cursin an liftin an swerrin

cause it takes too long
tae wait oan the craneman who
is lookin efter his mate
who stands him a few dinner-time bevies
at the Seven Seas public bar
an you know cause
that's wherr you get yir three pint chaser
fur yir ashet pie supper
that you eat wi yir rusty fingers,
then you fa oot wi the timekeeper
cause o the stupit time he pit oan the joab
an you kid oan the boey
who wiz daft enough tae
let yi pit a brush handle
through the arms of his ovies
an you play
spin the hammer
like it wiz yir prize six-shooter
an you laugh when the boey tries it
an it nearly brekks his toes,
an you go tae the burner
an patter him up
so he'll burn yir joab,
an you momentarily watch
his torch ignitin
an you watch
the gas you couldnae see
explodin
like a bomb,
an the cloud of rusty dust
an bodies hidin behind
guillotines an
flangers an
scrap buckets an
you squint through the haze
at the guy that's no therr
cause he's been blown down the passage
wi a hole in his side
that he didnae huv
before yi pattered him up,

an yi stoat ower tae the first aider
who pits a dod o cotton wool stuck oan
wi sellotape, ower yir eye,
an yi realise how lucky yi wur
an how lucky the burner wisnae,
then again,
he could have been the guy
that fell in the furnace,
the first aider wisnae much use tae him
neither he wiz.

Brian Whittingham, 1989

Church Unity Glasgow Style

The great ecumenical disaster of our time
Christian unity with a mohican haircut
And skinhead profile
Get the advocates of unitarianism
Batter the general council of world churches
Stamp oot the free thinkers
Mollacate the episcopacy of bishops
Integrate or annihilate
Show charity tae nane
It's either wedlock or the tomahawk
Whit'll it be jimmy.

William Gilfedder, 1989

from The Miracle of Glasgow's Cultural Revival (pre-1990)

In the Portakabin toilet (MEN)
on the south bank of the river (Clyde)
we harkened to a stubbled herald angel
who proclaimed:
'I think after Mayfest,
the Renfrew Ferry
will really take off.'

Douglas Lipton, 1990

The Thatcher Years

I

Stony rubbish, cruel months, fallen estates,
Possil, Gorbals, Drumchapel, Easterhouse,
Blackhill, heaps of broken images. Tiresias,
social worker in a combat jacket, gropes
blind in ugly closemouths, violent hours,
tumbling towerblocks, the battle scenes
perceived, foretells the rest with scribbled
case reports. Unreal City, between the giro
and the supersnoopers falls the shadow,
the pusher and the loan shark, the dead trees
that give no shelter twit jug twit jug.
Memories, desires, madly mix. Sweet Clyde,

run softly till I end my song, Sweet Clyde,
run softly, for I speak not loud or long.

II

The chair she sat in, like a burnt throne,
war words, her strange synthetic perfumes,
her red hair brushed out in fiery points.
Those are pearls that were her eyes. Fear
death by poverty, by the barbarous queen
so rudely forced. Do you know nothing? Do
you see nothing? Do you remember nothing?
'I remember all the streets savagely still,
Victorian family, solvent, virginal, around
the grand piano of the golden age empire.'
The fragments she has shored against her
ruin. Where the dead men lost their bones
she descends in a helicopter and still
she cries 'Jug jug' to shell-shocked ears.

III

The jobs have departed, leaving no addresses.
By the waters of the Clyde I sat down, wept
with all the gallus gluesniffers, hopeless, high,
heroin's heart beating a cool fool's retreat.
It riots and reigns in the junkie jungleland.
I had not thought smack had undone so many.
Unreal City, O City City I can sometimes hear
ancestral death-cries, Antony falling on his
sword, the pain of the hard man's poor wife.
This music crept by me upon the waters, left
me in the sweat of blood and tears, carried
through many vandalized halls, inexplicable
splendour, orange, green, white, gold, glisten.
In the DSS I can connect nothing with nothing.

IV

The burning burning burning burning middens
smoke me, choke me. Agonies in stony places.
A jessie rattles in a locked closet, done in.
That dream you planted last year in your
heart, has it begun to sprout? Will it bloom
this year? The wisest woman in all of Europe
deals her deadly pack, murderous jokers, open
season. Death on the rock. Bullets and gags.
You! Hypocrite with weird justice, odd peace
smelling of blood, tasting of fear. All profit
and loss, poor ends in the filthy whirlpool.
Suffer us not to mock ourselves with false
hood, a thousand nightmare launches. Lady, ten
Irishmen starved under your cruel iron rule.

V

After the coalmine black on sweaty faces,
after the echoes of plastic bullets that
ring in children's skulls, after the baton
charges, we who were living are now dying.
Who are those hooded hordes swarming over
endless streets, arid plains, with molotov
cocktails in the days of rage? Broadwater
Farm, Brixton, Belfast. The red sullen faces
sneer and snarl behind centurion shields.
Dixon of Dock Green with heavy truncheon.
O Lord thou fuckest me, crying 'You are here
to kneel.' Your creed's as cold as a slum's
pensioners in winter. I sat upon the shore
musing upon this thing my country's wreck.

John Maley, 1990

Great Western Road

Glasgow, you look beatific in blue
and I've a Saturday before me
for galleries and poems,
a house full of Haydn,
and beneath my kitchen window,
tennis stars in saris
lobbing backhands at the bins.
French coffee, and who knows maybe
Allen Ginsberg in my bath!
then round to the dairy
where scones are cooling on the rack
and Jimmy won't let me leave
till I've tried one there and then,
here, where the new Glasgow started –
an old grey city going blonde
whose Asian shops are full of fruits
we owe to Cap'n Bligh
and I'm so juiced I could walk clear
to Loch Lomond,
past buses stripping the willow
all along Great Western Road
but I just browse bargains in banjos
and pop art knitted ties,
before checking out the crime section
at Caledonian Books,
finding Freesias in the flowershops
and in the second-hand record store,
Bruckner's Third,
The Cleveland
under Szell:
so sad; like falling for passing students
with that black-haired, blue-eyed look,
or buying basil and chorizos . . .
In the afternoon I'll look at paintings

in Dougie Thomson's Mayfest show,
maybe stroll down to the studio
to view some archive film,
past the motorways and multi-storeys
of Grieve's Ultimate Cowcaddens,
the peeling pawn at George's Cross
where, today, everything is redeemable
because tonight there'll be guitar poets
from Russia at the Third Eye Centre.
And later I'll cook zarzuela
for a new and nimble friend.
God Glasgow it's glorious
just to gulp you down in heartfuls,
feeling something quite like love.

Donny O'Rourke, 1990

A City

– What was all that then? – What? – *That.* – That was *Glasgow.*
It's a film, an epic, lasts for, anyway
keep watching, it's not real, so everything is
melting at the edges and could go, you have to
remember some of it was shot in Moscow,
parts in Chicago, and then of course the people
break up occasionally, they're only graphics,
look there's two businessmen gone zigzag, they'll be
off-screen in one moment, yes, I thought so.
– What a sky though. – Ah well, the sky is listed,
change as it may. It's a peculiar platinum
with roary sunset flecks and fissures, rigging
was best against it, gone now, don't regret it,
move on, and if you wait you'll see some children,
oh it's a fine effect, maybe they're real, some

giant children pulling down a curtain
of platinum and scarlet stuff as airy
as it seems strong, and they'll begin to play there,
bouncing their shrill cries till it's too dark to
catch a shadow running along the backcloth,
and they still won't go home, despite the credits.
– You mean the film goes on, beyond the credits?
– You'll have to wait and see, won't you? It's worth it.
– I'm not persuaded even of its existence.
– What, *Glasgow?* – The city, not the film. – The city
is the film. – Oh come on. – I tell you. – Right then,
look. Renfield Street, marchers, banners, slogans.
Read the message, hear the chant. – Lights! Camera!
– But where are the children? – That I grant you;
somewhere, huge presences; shouting, laughter;
hunch-cuddy-hunch against a phantom housewall.

Edwin Morgan, 1990

Glasgow's Alive

Glasgow's alive and kicking,
Glasgow's alive and stabbing,
Glasgow's alive and shooting
Heroin into its veins.

Glasgow's alive and workless,
Glasgow's alive and poor,
Glasgow's alive and struggling
Tae keep the wolf fae the door.

Glasgow's alive and green,
Glasgow's alive and blue,

Gorbals (George Oliver)

Glasgow's alive and bigoted
Baith fenian and loyal and true.

Glasgow's alive and decadent,
Glasgow's alive and corrupt,
Glasgow's alive and exploited,
But her people will not be shut up.
So Glasgow's alive and flourishing,

Bells ringing, birds singing,
Fish swimming, trees growing,
In spite of the bastards.

Cath Craig, 1992

Gorbals, 1974 (George Oliver)

Briggait Steeple, Suspension Bridge, Jamaica Bridge and
Clyde Walkway, 1982 (George Oliver)

Notes

Glasgua (p.23)
The Scottish physician and poet Arthur Johnston wrote several Latin tributes to Scottish towns (*Economia Urbium*) which were collected posthumously in his *Poemata Omnia* (1642).

Glasgow (p.24)
This translation of Arthur Johnston's 'Glasgua' by John Barclay, minister of Cruden, appeared in *Memorialls For the Government of the Royall-Burghs in Scotland . . .* (Aberdeen: printed by John Forbes, 1685).

from **Glotta: A Poem** (p.25)
Printed in Glasgow by William Duncan. Not a lot is known about Arbuckle: he was a friend of Allan Ramsay and wrote a mock-heroic poem, 'Snuff', in 1719. 'Glotta' contains an interesting Popean description of golf on the Green.

John Highlandman's Remarks on the City of Glasgow (p.27)
Graham was bellman of Glasgow as well as a writer and seller of broadsides and chapbooks. This is an early example of a lowlander's fun at the expense of the supposed innocence and the imperfect English of Highlanders, many of whom had been flocking to the city in the wake of the '45. The Highlander thinks William III is a poor man because the statue is wearing Roman clothes. '. . . the deil chap the hours' is a reference to a clock in a Trongate clockmaker's window, on which a figure of the Devil struck the hours. The text here is taken from a chapbook of 1807 printed in Glasgow by J. & M. Robertson of Saltmarket.
See Alexander Fenton, 'The People Below: Dougal Graham's Chapbooks as a Mirror of the Lower Classes in Eighteenth-Century Scotland' in *A Day Estivall*, eds. Alisoun Gardner and James Hadley-Williams (Aberdeen University Press, 1990), pp.69–80.

from **Clyde: A Poem** (p.29)
Printed in Glasgow by Robert Urie. Wilson was a teacher; his last appointment was to Greenock Grammar School which he took up on condition he abandoned 'the profane and unprofitable art of poem-making'. In his poem on the Clyde he reveals himself as a good anti-Catholic Hanoverian. John Leyden edited the poem and added notes in his *Scotish Descriptive Poems* (1803).

The Cock-Sparrow and Goose, A Fable (p.31)
From *Miscellanies in Prose and Verse on Several Occasions* (4th ed., Edinburgh, 1771) which Wilson published under the pseudonym 'Claudero'. He lived in Edinburgh *c*.1750–90 and eked out a living as a satirist, campaigning, for example, to save old buildings from demolition. He made no great claims for his work: 'if the poems are lame, so is the author'.

Glasgow: A Poem (p.33)
From *The Glasgow Magazine and Review*, December 1783. Mayne called his poem 'the hasty effusion of the moment' and was later to expand it to sixty stanzas, with lengthy notes, in 1803. Written while he was apprenticed to the printer Andrew Foulis the younger.

Lunardi's Second Flight from Glasgow and **Glasgow Reviewed and Contrasted** (pp.37, 39)
From *Poems, Epistles and Songs, Chiefly in the Scottish Dialect* (Glasgow: printed by W. Bell for the author, 1788). Galloway was originally a shoemaker but found it too sedentary an

Burrell Gallery, 1983 (George Oliver)

Car showroom (George Oliver)

occupation, and became a bookseller and poet in Glasgow. Vincenzio Lunardi (1759–1806), the Italian balloonist, made two ascents by hydrogen balloon from Glasgow, both from St Andrew's Square. On the first, he landed at Hawick; on the second, at Campsie.

Verses on Viewing the Aqueduct Bridge (p.43)
From *Poetry Original and Selected*, vol.I (Glasgow: Brash and Reid, 1796). The Kelvin Aqueduct was built 1787–90 to carry the Forth and Clyde Canal over the Kelvin at Maryhill and was the largest canal aqueduct in Britain at that time.

Rab and Will, or The Twa Weavers *and* Song: The Fair (pp.45, 48)
From *Poems and Songs Chiefly in the Scottish Dialect* (Edinburgh: printed by J. Stark for the author, 1805). McIndoe was a silk loom weaver in Paisley and a hotel-keeper in Glasgow, a friend of Thomas Campbell, a fiddler and inventor of a machine for figuring muslin.

Captain Paton's Lament (p.50)
From *Blackwood's Magazine*, September 1819. Captain Archibald Paton (*d.*1807) was an eccentric (seen by Lockhart as a boy) who paraded the plainstanes at Glasgow Cross. The poem was reprinted in the third series of *Whistle-Binkie*, 1841.

Queer Folk at the Shaws (p.52)
Printed in Peter Mackenzie, *Glasgow Characters* (Glasgow: John Tweed, 1857). James McIndoe, an old soldier, was known as 'Jamie Blue' or 'Blue Thumbs' from his trade in selling indigo-coloured buttons. He also sold leeches, hardware and pepper, sang ballads and acted as town-crier. In an elegy in his *Poems* (Glasgow, 1845) Robert Husband describes him thus:

> Wi beard unshav'd, and poorly clad,
> Kilmarnock night-cap on his head,
> And over that, a bonnet braid, when seen at night,
> He, mair than ane come frae the dead, wad women fright.

There is another poem with a similar title, 'The Queer Folk in the Shaws' by James Fisher (*b.*1818, Glasgow), printed in Tom Leonard's *Radical Renfrew*; another version was put out by The Poet's Box in 1870.

Glasgow (p.53)
From the Glasgow periodical, the *Literary Reporter*, 1 March 1823. This was only Canto First of six – the rest has not been traced. '. . . the monument' refers to Nelson's Monument, erected on the Green in 1806.

Humours of Glasgow Fair (p.59)
From the *Literary Reporter*, 26 July 1823. The Fair was a popular subject: see also poems by Robert Galloway (in his *Poems*) and John Breckenridge (in Eyre-Todd, *The Glasgow Poets*). 'Shibboleth' here means the test to find out if a person is Irish: the pronunciation of words like tea and guinea.

Verses (p.71)
This happy vision of Glasgow's growth is taken from *The City Mirror; or Glasgow in Miniature* (Glasgow, 1824). Harriston was a jack-of-all-trades (weaver, soldier, fisherman, pedlar) who hawked his poems (autobiographical verses and commentaries on the passing scene) on the streets and quays. He also wrote *The Steam-Boat Traveller's Remembrancer* (1824) and a Glaswegian version of Gray's *Elegy* ('The bell has toll'd the hour of closing shops').

Saturday in Glasgow (p.73)
From *Poems* . . . (Glasgow: printed for the widow of the author by William Eadie & Co, 1860). Watt was a handloom weaver. All his poems were written before 1831, the year he married. The 'sinfu' cargo' in stanza three refers to the practice of watering the milk on its way into Glasgow from the country.

Lines on Revisiting a Scottish River (p.80)
This piece of nostalgia was written when Campbell, who had left Glasgow in 1797 at the age of twenty, returned in 1827 as Lord Rector of Glasgow University, revisiting his childhood haunts and lamenting the changes. From *Poetical Works* (London: Moxon, 1854).

Know ye the town . . . (p.82)
Student satire from the Glasgow magazine, the *Athenaeum*, 1830. Quoted in J. A. Hammerton, *Sketches from Glasgow* (1893).

Petition (p.83)
From *Poems and Songs* (Glasgow: David Robertson, 1838). Rodger was variously a silversmith, weaver, music teacher, cloth inspector and pawnbroker (as in the poem); he also suffered imprisonment for his radical activities. The dyeworks he is so anxious to return to is the Barrowfield Dyeworks. *Poems and Songs* also includes his 1818 satirical poem on the new savings banks, 'Shaving Banks'. His poems are collected in *Poems and Songs*, ed. Robert Ford (Paisley and London: Alexander Gardner, 1901).

Sanct Mungo (p.84)
This pastiche, originally set to music and arranged as a glee for three voices by John Turnbull, is from Rodger's *Poems and Songs* (1838). An earlier version appeared in the first series of *Whistle-Binkie*, 1832.

Yes, yon fair town (p.86)
This bleak vision of a future Glasgow is from *The Bard of the North: A Series of Poetical Tales, Illustrative of Highland Scenes and Character* (Glasgow: David Robertson, 1833). Moore was a copperplate printer turned bookseller, encouraged by the Glasgow publisher James Lumsden. He was bled to death by his doctor who was treating him for a slight inflammation.

from **The Weaver's Saturday: A Political Poem** (p.87)
Printed in Glasgow by W. & W. Miller. The author of this urban version of 'The Cottar's Saturday Night' has been identified (by the French scholar Hugues Journès) as the Glasgow Chartist weaver poet George Donald (1801–51). However, the English historian of radical poetry, Jim Clayson, has argued persuasively against this attribution, although he has been unable to come up with an alternative. One thing is certain – the poem was written by a weaver.

Let Glasgow Flourish! (p.95)
From *Songs* (Glasgow: Richard Griffin, 1842). Park was an unsuccessful teacher, hat salesman and bookseller (he bought Dugald Moore's business after his death). 'A gentleman at large, existing by his wits, and courted for his society' (Charles Rogers).

Glasgow (p.96)
A sonnet from *The Necropolis: An Elegy and other poems* (Glasgow: David Bryce, 1842). Mary Waugh was the widow of James Macarthur, merchant in Glasgow.

St Rollox Lum's Address to its Brethren (p.96)
Mitchell was a Paisley shoemaker, poet and political pamphleteer. Built in 1842, at about 450 feet, 'Tennant's Stalk' was the tallest chimney in Europe (until surpassed fifteen years later by Townsend's chimney), carrying away the noxious fumes (or 'sooty treasures' as a contemporary put it) of Charles Tennant's St Rollox chemical works. Thomson, McIntyre & Co were the builders of the chimney. The poem was first printed in the Glasgow Liberal newspaper, the *Argus*, and in the *Reformers' Gazette* in 1842, and reprinted in Mitchell's *My Grey Goose Quill* (Paisley: Caldwell & Son, 1852), from which the text is taken.

from **Wee Charlie's Elegy** (p.102)
From *Lays of St Mungo*, ed. James Lemon (Glasgow: Smith & Watson, 1844). Lemon worked in the Glasgow Post Office for over forty years. Charles Cochran was a lamplighter in

Glasgow for nearly fifty years; he was known for the way he shovelled snuff into his nose and for frightening wee boys, telling them he was 'the seventh son o' the seventh dochter'.

from **How We Spent a Sabbath Day** (p.104)
Published as a pamphlet 'by a Working Man, for the members of the Sabbath Alliance' (Glasgow: printed by Campbell & Co, *c.*1846). The Glasgow and Edinburgh Railway, which opened in 1842, ran on Sundays. The poem is a Christian response to the outcry this occasioned. See also Alexander Rodger's poem 'Sunday Railway Trains' (in his collected *Poems and Songs*, 1901).

The Street and **A Tale of the Town** (pp.113, 115)
From *City Songs* (Glasgow: Thomas Murray, 1855). Macfarlan is unjustly neglected. Despite the influence of Alexander Smith (as in these poems), he is of interest in his own right. He lived and died in poverty, spent what money he earned on drink, scribbled in taverns and bit any hand that tried to feed him. His work appeared in a variety of pamphlets and journals (including Dickens's *All the Year Round*); his poem 'The Lords of Labour' was particularly admired by Thackeray. See Hamish Whyte, 'The Miseries of Hope: James Macfarlan (1832–1862)' in *A Glasgow Collection*, eds. Kevin McCarra and Hamish Whyte (Glasgow: Glasgow City Libraries, 1990), pp.137–55.

from **The Wanderer** (p.117)
Published in Glasgow by Thomas Murray and in London by Arthur Hall, Virtue & Co.

Glasgow and *from* **A Boy's Poem** (pp.117, 122)
From *City Poems* (Cambridge: Macmillan, 1857). An earlier version of 'Glasgow', 'To a City', had appeared in the *Glasgow University Album* for 1854, and first appeared in this form in the *Scotsman*, 19 August 1857.

The Gallant Shoemakers and **Glasgow Fair** (pp.123, 124)
These songs were printed and sold (for 1d) by Matthew Leitch at The Poet's Box, 6 St Andrews Lane, Gallowgate. The first was written by 'a worthy member of the craft who along with his brethren struck work on Tuesday, 6th May, 1857, for an advance of wages'. The second is by William Burns, 'a very young man . . . of East Kilbride', otherwise unknown. There are 3,000 such songs in the Mitchell Library's Glasgow Collection, printed on flimsy sheets of paper 10 × 4 inches, with the words of 2,975 songs, hundreds of them with a Glasgow setting: Adam McNaughtan has provided a subject index to them. They deserve a separate selection.

Heaven Knows (p.126)
From *Poems and Essays*, second edition (Glasgow: Thomas Murray, 1863), and differs little from the version in the first edition of 1863, apart from the addition of the title and tidied-up punctuation. Janet Hamilton of Coatbridge wrote on current local and national events that came under her shrewd consideration; her poems in Scots are particularly lively. Here she has no doubt that Madeleine Smith murdered her lover, Pierre L'Angelier – the verdict in this famous trial of 1857 was Not Proven. The island is Jersey, L'Angelier's birthplace. The Glasgow poisoner William Pritchard was also the subject of a poem at his trial eight years later, by Anon.: 'Dr Pritchard Turned into a Pillar of Salt' (Glasgow: Gage & Gray, 1865) – 'Deals out the poisoned cheese, egg-flip, and wine, / And, smiling, says, "My darling, it is fine!" '

Lightburn Glen (p.127)
From *Scottish Nursery Songs, And Other Poems* (Glasgow: Kerr & Richardson, 1863) which includes Miller's most famous poem, 'Willie Winkie' which had first appeared in the third series of *Whistle-Binkie*, 1841.

Let Glasgow Flourish (p.128)
From *Lyrics and Ballads* (Glasgow: David Robertson, 1863). Originally from Kilwinning, Manson worked on the *Glasgow Herald*.

from **A Welcome to the Waters of Loch-Katrine** (p.131)
In *Kilwuddie and other poems* (Glasgow: Scottish Temperance League, 1863). Nicholson, foreman tailor at Govan Workhouse, was considered the laureate of the temperance movement. This evangelical paean to Glasgow's water was suggested by the sight of water rising from a burst pipe in the street. The Water Works, supplying the city from the Perthshire loch, were opened in 1859 (at a total cost of £1,500,000).

from **My New Location** (p.133)
This appeared in Young's *Homely Pictures* (Glasgow: George Gallie, 1865) and is addressed to Janet Hamilton, in imitation of her poem 'Oor Location' (in her *Poems and Essays*, 1863). His new location is 3 Swan Street, Port Dundas. As an inmate of Barnhill Poorhouse (where he ended up after an accident had maimed and nearly blinded him) he had published *Lays from the Poorhouse* in 1860 which attracted favourable notice and 'generous patrons' enabled him to leave and settle in 'domestic felicity'.

Dedicated to the People of Glasgow (p.135)
From *Original Poetry* (Glasgow: Porteous Brothers, 1865). One of the many voices of the time clamouring for something to be done about Glasgow's dreadful housing conditions. In 1866 the City Improvement Act inaugurated the demolition and replacement of large areas of substandard housing. Pearson was also the author of *An Analysis of the Human Mind* (London, 1863).

Address to the Factory of Messrs J. & W. I. Scott & Co (p.139)
From *Poems and Songs* (Glasgow: William Love, 1867). Ellen Johnston achieved a brief fame as the 'Poetical Factory Girl'. She died in the Barony Poorhouse. The poem paints a slightly idealised picture of the factory of James and William Inglis Scott, cotton spinners and power-loom cloth manufacturers, Bridgeton.

Wanted in Glasgow and **A Song of Glasgow Town** (p.141, 142)
From *Mirren's Musings* (Glasgow: McGeachy & M. Bernstein, 1876). Marion Bernstein was a music teacher, housebound owing to a contraction of the sciatic nerve. She nevertheless kept up a lively interest in passing events and commented on them in witty, feminist poems in the *Weekly Mail*.

First Fittin' (p.143)
From *The Blinkin' o' the Fire* (Glasgow: Cossar, Fotheringham & Co, 1877). Jessie Russell was a dressmaker who married a ship's carpenter in 1873. Her poems appeared in the local press along with Marion Bernstein's.

Ayrshire Jock (p.145)
Published in *In a Music Hall and Other Poems* (London: Ward and Downey, 1891) but written well before Davidson left Scotland in 1889.

from **A Hundred Years Ago** (p.149)
This poem celebrated the centenary of the *Glasgow Herald*, February 1882.

Iron Shipbuilding on the Clyde, The Clyde and **Doon the Watter at the Fair** (pp.150, 151, 153)
From *Songs and Poems* (Glasgow: Andrew Cochrane, 1888). Kennedy seems to have been a kind of poet laureate of the Govan area, commenting on events and writing for local functions. See also 'Down the Water' by Patrick Buchan in *Whistle-Binkie*, second series (Glasgow: David Robertson, 1842).

Glasgow (p.154)
From *Poetic Gems* (Dundee, 1890). Written in 1889 while McGonagall was in Glasgow: 'I was treated like a prince, but owing to declining health I had to leave.'

Ode to the Clyde (p.156)
First appeared in *Glasgow University Magazine*; reprinted in *Glasgow University Verses 1903–1910* and in Kirk's *Clyde Ballads* (Glasgow: Hodge, 1911). Written in the cage of a buoy moored in the Clyde off Cardross.

Breathes There a Man –? (p.157)
From *The Outpost*, August 1915, the magazine of the 17th (Service) Battalion Highland Light Infantry. This piece of wartime nostalgia (which milks Glasgow place-names for all they are worth) was written from training camp in Yorkshire, just before setting off for France and the Somme. Reprinted in *Battalion Ballads* (Glasgow: D. J. Clark, 1916). Hutcheson was a civil engineer who served his apprenticeship at Fairfield. See article in *Scots Magazine* vol.58, 1952, pp.129–35.

In Glasgow (p.158)
From MacDiarmid's first collection of poems, *Sangschaw* (Edinburgh: Blackwood, 1925). F. G. Scott is the poet's friend, the composer Francis George Scott. The Cowcaddens was one of the most densely populated districts in Glasgow, polluted by local industry and with a high concentration of pubs.

Symbol (p.158)
From the *Scots Observer*, 10 November 1932. '. . . they iron banes' – work on No. 534, John Brown's, the *Queen Mary*, was suspended, at the height of the Depression, and the ship was left on the stocks from 1931 until 1934.

Glasgow Street (p.159)
Originally appeared, with different lineation, in *Via* (London: Boriswood, 1933).

Industrial Scene (p.159)
Taken from the Glasgow section of Muir's *Scottish Journey* (London: Heinemann/Gollancz, 1935; reissued by Mainstream, 1979). Muir wrote: 'as I can speak with no exact knowledge of the rich of Glasgow, I shall give instead a short poem which took shape during my journey through the industrial regions, and arose from a sense of the violent contrasts that I saw on every side.' (p.152.) Also published in *Time and Tide*, 9 March 1935, with slightly different text, and finally collected in *The Complete Poems of Edwin Muir*, ed. Peter Butter (Aberdeen: Association for Scottish Literary Studies, 1991).

Glasgow 1960 (p.160)
First printed in the *London Mercury*, December 1935, but not collected until the *Collected Poems* of 1962.

Twin-Screw Set – 1902 (p.161)
From *Chota Chants* (Glasgow: Fraser, Edward & Co, 1937).

The City Cemetery (p.163)
Cernuda lived in Glasgow from 1939 until 1943, working as a lecturer at the University. 'Cementerio de la Ciudad' was first published in *Las nubes* (Buenos Aires, 1943). Edwin Morgan translated the poem in 1956 – see his *Rites of Passage* (Carcanet, 1976). This version is from Ron Butlin's collection, *Creatures Tamed by Cruelty* (Edinburgh: EUSPB, 1979) and first published in *New Edinburgh Review* 45, February 1979, as 'The Glasgow Cemetery'.

Whose Children? (p.164)
From *When Sleeps the Tide* (Glasgow: the author, 1943). Hunter came from a Lanarkshire mining family, emigrated to New Zealand (where he was known as the songwriter 'Billy

Banjo'), returned to Scotland, worked as a journalist and represented the Cowcaddens ward as a Labour councillor from 1937 until his death in 1959.

from Setterday Nicht Symphonie and A Glesca Rhapsodie (pp.167, 169)

These lively idiosyncratic Scots poems are taken from *Fowrsom Reel* (Glasgow: Caledonian Press, 1949), a collection by Kincaid and three other poets, George Todd, Freddie J. Anderson and Thurso Berwick (Morris Blythman) who constituted the 'Clyde Group'. Their aim, in Hamish Henderson's words, was 'to produce work which [would] interpret more immediately the reality of the Scottish people' (*Our Time*, September 1949, p.305). 'Setterday Nicht Symphonie' first appeared in MacDiarmid's magazine, *Voice of Scotland*, June 1948.

News of the World (p.171)

Based on a memory of reading a news item in the *Daily Record* about 1930 and coloured by Lorca's poem of a few years earlier, 'Muerte de Antoñito el Camborio', about a clan fight on the banks of the Guadalquivir.

Perishin' Poem (p.175)

The text as it first appeared on the front page of the *Evening Times*, 1 December 1952, with no accompanying cartoon.

The Labour Provost (p.175)

From *The Rebels Ceilidh Song Book*, reprinted in *Workers City*, ed. Farquhar McLay (Glasgow: Clydeside Press, 1988). The provost is allegedly Sir Patrick Dollan, Lord Provost 1938–41.

Sràid ann an Glaschu (Street in Glasgow) (p.178)

From *Saltire Review*, Spring 1956. Included in *Eadar Samradh is Foghar* (Glasgow: Gairm, 1967).

Glasgow Beasts (p.180)

First published by the Wild Hawthorn Press, with illustrations from papercuts by John Picking and Pete McGinn.

Cod Liver Oil and Orange Juice (p.183)

Also known as 'Hairy Mary' or 'Hairy Mary and the Hardman'.

King Billy and Glasgow Green (pp.184, 186)

From the group of Edwin Morgan's Glasgow poems written between April 1962 and September 1964. Others are 'Linoleum Chocolate', 'Trio', 'The Starlings in George Square' and 'In the Snack-Bar'. Morgan described these as 'about simple things happening in Glasgow to me or other people or about things I read about in the paper'. They can all be found in his *Collected Poems* (Manchester: Carcanet, 1990).

glasgow's full of artists (p.188)

From *All Fall Down* (Edinburgh: Kelvin Press, 1965).

Six Glasgow Poems (p.188)

The first of these to appear in print was 'The Good Thief', in *Scottish International* 1, January 1968. They are included with Tom Leonard's other work in *Intimate Voices* (Newcastle upon Tyne: Galloping Dog Press, 1984).

The Coming of the Wee Malkies (p.191)

First published in *Glasgow University Magazine*, Whitsun 1967, as winner of fourth place in the BBC Scottish Home Service University Notebook Poetry Competition.

The Jeely Piece Song (p.192)
Also known as 'The Height Starvation Song'. Printed with music in the *Scottish Folksinger* (London: Collins, 1973).

Glasgow, Easter 1968 (p.193)
From *Words* 7, 1979.

Glasgow (p.194)
From *The Most Difficult Area* (London: Cape Goliard Press, 1968).

the docks on Sunday (p.195)
From *Glasgow University Magazine*, 80:3, 1969.

Rider (p.196)
First published in *Scottish International* 8, November 1969. Appropriately for this anthology it is about Glasgow poets past and present.

The Butchers of Glasgow (p.200)
This poem and many of McGinn's songs and stories are collected in *McGinn of the Calton* (Glasgow: Glasgow District Libraries, 1987).

Glasgow and You Lived in Glasgow (p.201)
From *Lines Review*, 29, June 1969, and *Love Poems and Elegies* (London: Gollancz, 1972) respectively. Both are included in *Collected Poems* (Manchester: Carcanet, 1992).

An Glaschu (In Glasgow) (p.204)
No.35 in the sequence *An Rathad Cian* (Glasgow: Gairm, 1970).

In Glasgow (p.206)
From *Twelve Songs* (West Linton: Castlelaw Press, 1970).

Nostalgie (p.206)
In *Poems* (Preston: Akros Publications, 1971).

Obituary (p.208)
First published in the Glasgow University Extra Mural magazine EMU 1, 1971, and included as were **Something I'm Not** (under the title 'Local Colour') and **Carnival** in *Memo for Spring* (Edinburgh: Reprographia, 1972), Liz Lochhead's first collection. All are included in *Dreaming Frankenstein & Collected Poems* (Edinburgh: Polygon Books, 1984).

A Dug A Dug (p.210)
From *Glasgow University Magazine*, 82:3, 1971. Reprinted in *The Scottish Dog*, eds. J. and M. Lindsay (Aberdeen: Aberdeen University Press, 1989).

Glasgow Sonnets (p.212)
Written 2–10 January 1972 and issued as a pamphlet by the Castlelaw Press in May of that year.

Lament for a Lost Dinner Ticket (p.216)
This now legendary poem was first published in *Scottish International*, April 1972.

from **A Sense of Order** and **Family Visit** (pp.220, 221)
From *An Ear to the Ground* (London: Hutchinson, 1972).

Seen Out (p.223)
In *Aquarius* 6, 1973. Reprinted in *Collected Poems 1940–1990* (Edinburgh: Mercat Press).

The Girl I Met in Byres Road (p.224)
From *Poems* (York: Eboracum, 1973).

there was that time charlie tully (p.224)
From *Aquarius* 6, 1973.

On John Maclean (p.225)
First published in *Homage to John Maclean* (Glasgow: John Maclean Society, 1973), which also gives sources for the quotations in the poem.

By the Preaching of the Word (p.227)
In Hayden Murphy's Dublin magazine *Broadsheet* 21, June 1974.

Pigeons in George Square (p.228)
In *Aquarius* 7, 1974.

Tea Time (p.228)
From *Bunnit Husslin* (Glasgow: Third Eye Centre, 1975) and reprinted in *Intimate Voices*.

To Lesbia's Husband (p.229)
From *Oasis* 1, 1975. Some of Neilson's Glaswegian translations from Catullus were collected in *XII from Catullus* (Glasgow: Mariscat Press, 1982).

Gorbals (p.229)
In *Akros* 37, April 1977.

The Bargain (p.230)
First published in *Asphalt Garden*, 4, 1977. Collected in *Dreaming Frankenstein & Collected Poems* (Edinburgh: Polygon Books, 1984).

Ghosts (p.233)
From *Under the Ice* (London: Hutchinson, 1978).

Glasgow (p.234)
From *Scottish Review* 15, August 1979. In MacDiarmid's poem 'Glasgow' (*Voice of Scotland*, June 1947, and *Noise and Smoky Breath*, 1983) he had written 'The houses are Glasgow, not the people'.

Glasgow, 1956 (p.237)
In *New Edinburgh Review*, Winter 1980. Collected in *Waiting for the Storm* (Newcastle upon Tyne: Bloodaxe Books, 1990).

Jingle (p.238)
From the pamphlet *Glasgow Zen* (Glasgow: Glasgow Print Studio, 1982).

Sometimes it's Hard to be a Woman (p.240)
From the revue *Tickly Mince*, written with Alasdair Gray and Tom Leonard. Collected in *True Confessions & New Clichés* (Edinburgh: Polygon Books, 1985).

Clydegrad and Matt McGinn (pp.241, 242)
From the post-1979 sequence *Sonnets from Scotland* (Glasgow: Mariscat Press, 1984).

Parachuting into Glasgow (p.242)
In the short-lived *Glasgow Magazine* 5, 1984/85.

A Glasgow Cassandra (p.243)
A selection of Mulrine's translations from Ronsard appeared in *Chapman* 40, Spring 1985.

Gunfight at the Govan Corral (p.244)
Collected in *Waiting for the Storm*. In the *Glasgow Herald*, 4 February 1989.

You have returned to Glasgow after a long exile (p.246)
From *Situations Theoretical and Contemporary* (Newcastle upon Tyne: Galloping Dog Press, 1986).

James Maxton (p.246)
From *Chapman* 47–48, Spring 1987 (Tom Scott issue).

Plain Speaking (p.247)
From *New Writing Scotland 6* (Aberdeen: Association for Scottish Literary Studies, 1988).

Birds of Passage (p.248)
From *Cencrastus* 25, Spring 1987.

Kelvinbridge: A Node (p.249)
In *Verse*, November 1988.

Inner Glasgow (p.252)
In Robert Crawford's first collection, *A Scottish Assembly* (London: Chatto & Windus, 1990).

Joan Eardley (p.253)
From *Cencrastus* 32, New Year 1989. Tribute to two of the artist's main subjects: tenement life and seascape. See also poems by Edwin Morgan and Tom Scott.

Carbolic Dan (p.254)
Previously unpublished.

The Journeyman (p.254)
From *London Toes* (Renfrew: Crazy Day Press, 1989).

Church Unity Glasgow Style (p.256)
From *New Writing Scotland 7* (Aberdeen: ASLS, 1989).

from **The Miracle of Glasgow's Cultural Revival (pre-1990)** (p.257)
From *West Coast Magazine* 5, June 1990.

The Thatcher Years (p.257)
From *Scream, If You Want To Go Faster* (Aberdeen: ASLS, 1991) (*New Writing Scotland 9*).

Great Western Road (p.260)
From *Scream, If You Want To Go Faster* (1991).

A City (p.261)
In *Hold Hands Among the Atoms* (Glasgow: Mariscat Press, 1991).

Glasgow's Alive (p.262)
From *Slip Roads & Off Ramps: Writing from Castlemilk*, ed. Dilys Rose (Glasgow: Cutting Teeth, 1992).

Glossary

(Includes names and places)

abune	above	belyve	soon
ae	one	ben	in, inside
ahint	behind	bicker	beaker
airt	art	bien	comfortable
airtin	making one's way	bigg	build
airts	directions, points of	billies	lads, fellows
	the compass	bing	heap, pile
Arcadian	of Arcadia, fabled	birkies	smart fellows
	pastoral area of	birlin'	hurrying along,
	Greece		whirling
asteer	in a commotion	Blackhill	housing scheme in
Athole brose	honey or oatmeal		north of city
	mixed with whisky	blate	bashful, timid,
athort	all over, in every		modest
	direction	bloo'er	smash
atweel	certainly, indeed	blye	blithe
aucht	anything, nothing	bogey, the gemme's	
ayont	beyond	a	stalemate
		bonny-clabber	milk curdled
bailie	magistrate		naturally
barley-bree	whisky	bosie	bosom
Barnhill	poorhouse, near	brag	challenge
	Springburn	braird	sprout
Barrhead	town, south-west of	braw	fine, splendid,
	Glasgow		excellent
baw	ball	braws	fine clothes
bawbee	halfpenny	bree	juice, broth
Bearsden	posh district,	broads	shutters
	north-west of	broo	social security
	Glasgow		office (bureau)
beelan	festering	Broomielaw	Glasgow quay,
beet	relieve, comfort,		embarkation point
	help		for pleasure
beil'	shelter, refuge		steamers
Bel-'e Brae	Bell o' the Brae,	Brunswick	George III
	part of the High	buffed	laughed aloud
	Street	buffin	coarse cloth
belly-flaught	flat on one's face or	bum-flees	bluebottles
	stomach	bummel	blunderer

Burdett	Sir Francis Burdett (1770–1844), popular English politician	cleed	clothe
		cleedin'	clothing
		cleekit	linked arms
burns, made their	urinated	Cleghorn	Dr Robert Cleghorn, physician at Royal Infirmary
burnty	burned-out house		
		Cleland, Baillie	James Cleland, Master of Works
Calderpark	Glasgow zoo		
caller	fresh	Clenny	Cleansing Department
Calton	east end district		
Campsies	range of hills north of Glasgow	cloks	beetles
		clour	lump caused by a blow
Candleriggs	street near old city centre		
		clout	cloth, rag, duster
Canicular	dog-days, hottest part of the year	Clutha	Clyde
		cog	bowl
canny	gentle, steady, good	Corcyran	of Corfu
cantie	cheerful; small and neat	core	convivial group
		Corkindale	Dr James Corkindale, physician, 156 Saltmarket
carlin	old woman; witch		
Carntyne	district in east of city		
Carrick	area of Ayrshire	corse	cross
Castlemilk	housing scheme in south of city	coup'd	fell over; upended into
caurs	cars (often tramcars)	cout	awkward person; an adolescent
causey	road, pavement	couthie	friendly, agreeable
Cessnock	underground station south of the river	Cowal	district of Argyll, between Firth of Clyde and Loch Fyne
changehouse	inn, alehouse		
chap	knock	Cowcaddens	district north of city centre
chapin	chopin, a measure of about two pints		
		crack	talk, gossip
chiel	fellow, man	cracket	talked, chatted
chinas	mates	Craig	possibly William Craig of Paisley, d.1829
chirted	squeezed, pressed		
choud	?stew		
chuckies	small stones, pebbles	craw	crow (shoot the craw – leave)
clachan	village	crimpy cakes	?crumpets
clawcht	caught	criple	hobble
clawts	hoes; implements for scraping dung	Crossmyloof	south-side district
		crottlan	covered with lichen

crouse	spirited, merry	dunnerin'	thundering
cuddies	donkeys, horses	dunny	lower back passage
cuff'd	removed		(of close)
cut-and-dry	cut and dried	dwaum, dwam	stupor, daydream
	tobacco	dwine	fade, waste away
cutty stoup	pewter vessel	dyke	wall
	holding one eighth	dyvours	debtors
	of a chopin		
		Eardley, Joan	Sussex-born
dang	*see* ding		Glasgow artist
daud	lump, large piece		(1921–63)
daw	dawn	Easterhouse	housing scheme in
deavsome	annoying		east of city
deed-thraws	death throes	Ecclefechan	village in
deleerit	delirious, out of		Dumfriesshire
	one's senses	eekit	filled
Denny-Palais	Dennistoun Palais	een	eyes
	(de Danse), in east	eident	industrious,
	of Glasgow		diligent
desavin	deceiving	eke	supplement,
didgy	dustbin		improve
dights	gives a quick wash	ell	Scots ell, four fifths
ding	beat, strike, drive,		of English
	dash		measurement
dirl	rattle		
doilt	weary; stupid	fabs	fobs
doitet	foolish	fairheid	fairhead
dounset	laying-low	fash	trouble, bother
doup	buttocks	feck	a great many; the
dree	endure, suffer		majority
dreep	let oneself down (a	feet up	expression used by
	wall, usually)		carters when a
	hanging at full		horse stumbles
	arms' stretch	fel	feel
dreich, dreigh	dreary	fend	sustenance
dressing	the prepared web	ferlies	strange sights;
	(in weaving)		gossip
drouthy	thirsty	fidges	fidgets
drowie	misty	fient	the devil . . .
Drumchapel	housing scheme in	Finnieston	district beside
	north-west of city		River Clyde west of
drumlie	disturbed, troubled;		Broomielaw
	clouded	Firre Parke	Fir Park, where the
dught	could		Necropolis now is
dunch'd	nudged	fleyt	scared

flichterin	fluttering, rushing about excitedly	gralloch	disembowel
flints	journeymen who refused to comply with employers' terms (orig. of tailors)	Gray, David	poet (1838–61) from Kirkintilloch, near Glasgow
		greet	cry, lament
		grieve	foreman
		Grosvenor	city centre restaurant
fly	cunning, devious		
flytes	scolds	grues	shudders, shrieks in horror
fou	full; drunk		
furbye	beyond	grumly	unsettled
fyle	to soil	gudesake	for God's sake
gab	gob, mouth	haar	mist
Gallacher	William Gallacher (1881–1967), Red Clydesider	haflin	half-grown boy, adolescent
		hained	kept unused
Gallowgate	road east of Glasgow Cross	haith	exclamation of surprise
gallus	bold, tough, sharp	hallan	inner partition between door and fireplace
gars	makes		
gash	smart		
gate	journey	hanselt	fr. han[d]sel, to inaugurate with ceremony or gift to bring good luck; to use for the first time
gaunts	stammers		
gawsy	cocky, jolly		
Gilmorehill	site of Glasgow University in west of city		
gin	if	hap	call to horses, esp. in ploughing to turn right
glaikit	stupid, foolish		
glar, glaur	mud, muck		
Glasgow magistrates	plump red herrings	harns	brains
		hauf-bilet	half-boiled
glaumerie	enchantment, magic	heddles	cords through which the warp is passed in a loom after going through the reed, by means of which the warp threads are separated into two sets to allow the passage of the shuttle with the weft
gleed	mistaken, awry		
gleg	sharp, keen, quick		
glinkan	glancing, peeping		
glinks	glances, gives a sidelong look		
Gorbals	district south of the river		
gowan	daisy		
gowks	fools		
graith	soapy lather; equipment, uniform		

heich	high	Kelvinside	posh west end
heidies	street football game		district
	(also headers)	Kibble Palace	large glasshouse in
hems, pit the, oan	put out of action,		Botanic Gardens
	contain	kilts	tucks up
hink	think	kimmers	wives
hinnie	honey	Kinawl	Canal (Monkland)
hizzies	women	kitchen'd	flavoured, seasoned
howked	dug		
hunch–cuddy–		lair	lore, learning
hunch	children's team	lather	ladder
	game	lay	framed part of the
Hunter, Samuel	editor of the		loom which strikes
	Glasgow Herald		home each
hurdies	buttocks, hips		successive weft
			thread; the batten
ilk	each	leal	faithful, loyal;
ilka	every		chaste
Ixion	mythical Lapith	lear	muck
	king bound to	leerie	lamplighter
	revolving wheel of	leids	lads
	fire in hell	lift	sky
		limmer	mistress, whore
jaur	jar	loaby	lobby
jile	jail	loan	street
jobbernowl	blockhead	lone	lane
jocteleg	clasp-knife	loun	rascal
jorum	large drinking	loun[e]	grassy cattle track;
	bowl, esp. of punch		pasture
jouk'd	flickered; dodged	lourd	heavy, sluggish
		loused	loosed
kail	cabbage broth	lowe	fire
keel	mark made with	lowpan	leaping
	ruddle by warper at	lowsan	releasing
	each end of warp to	luckies	things found by
	ensure that weaver		luck
	returns the correct	lug	ear
	amount of woven	lum	chimney
	thread	lyfts	skies
keezened	dry, shrivelled		
kelt	homespun black or	MacBrayne	steamer company
	grey cloth	Maclean, John	Glasgow Socialist
Kelvin	tributary of Clyde		Republican (1879–
Kelvinhaugh	district on north		1923)
	bank of Clyde	maen	moan

mankie	calamanco, a glossy woollen material	New Street	now King Street, near Glasgow Cross
mattam	pseudo-Highland form of madam	nowt	ox; oaf, clumsy person; nought, nothing
maun	must		
maun'd	managed		
mawin	cutting	ohon	alas
Maxton, James	ILP MP for Bridgeton (1885–1946)	Paestum	ancient coastal town of southern Italy, famous for roses
meikle	much		
mell	mingle, mix		
mense	dignity	pakes	just deserts
Menstra Green	?Menstrie, Stirlingshire	pan	toilet
		pang	stuff, gorge
Millguy	local pronunciation of Milngavie, posh district north-west of Glasgow	Paphos	city of Cyprus, where Venus was worshipped
		Para Handy	captain of west coast puffer in stories by Neil Munro
minny	affectionate name for mother		
mirk	darkness, night; dark, gloomy	paraletic	falling-down drunk
Monklan	Monkland Canal, between Forth and Clyde Canal at Port Dundas and North Calder Water in Lanarkshire	Partick	district in west of Glasgow
		pat	pot
		patir	patter, chat
		Peterhead	Aberdeenshire fishing village and prison
Mount Vernon	district to east of Glasgow	pew	puff
muckle	great	pewed	cried like a bird
		philabeg	kilt
nab	person of importance or wealth; snob	piece	sandwich or slice of bread spread with jam etc
nainsel	one's own self; used as nickname: 'her nainsel' = a Highlander	pirn	bobbin
		plankt	hidden
		Plantation St	in Govan, on south side of river
nappy	strong ale	plisky	trick
Nassau	William III	plouks	boils, pimples
neeves	fists	pooch	pocket
neist	next		
neivfu'	handful		

Porteous, Dr	Rev William Porteous (1735–1812) of St George's Tron	sannies	sandshoes, plimsolls
		sappy	succulent, plump
		sapsy	soft, soppy
Possilpark	district in north of Glasgow	Sauchiehall	one of Glasgow's main shopping streets
pree, prie	sample		
preens	pins	scabbit	scabbed
pricket	fastened	scart	scratch
propine	outlay	scawt	scabby, scruffy, shabby
puirtith	poverty		
		Schipka Pass	short street off Gallowgate
ram stam	headlong, heedlessly	schunner	scunner
raucle	hard, grim, rough	screed	scratch
rax't	grew	screwtaps	beer bottles with screw tops
ree	tipsy, over-excited		
reek	smoky	scud	beat, skip across
remeid	remedy, redress	scunner	feeling of disgust, distaste, aversion
rerr	rare		
retour	return, way back; return journey by carriage	shap	blow
		shauchlin	shuffling
		Shaws	Pollokshaws, village on the south side
reuch	rough		
Rodney	Lord Rodney (1719–92), English admiral	Shettleston	district in east of Glasgow
		shielin	hut
roul-poul	form of ninepins played at fairs	shoogly	swaying, wobbling
		sidelins	sideways
routh	crowd, plenty; abundant	sinsyne	since then
		skailan	dispersing
ruff	drumming of feet on floor as expression of applause	skeich	spirited
		skelping	getting up to mischief
		skelps	smacks, blows
ruggs	tugs	skirls	screeches
ruise	to praise	skite	slap, blow
rummlan	rumbling	sklents	glances sideways, looks askance
rumps	cuts, crops		
Rutherglen	burgh south-east of Glasgow, now part of city	skytin'	shooting through the air
		slee	sly
		sleekit	smooth, sly, plausible
Saccharissa	Sweetest		
sair	serve	slevvery	wet, damp

282

smouchteran	smoking, smouldering	Tannahill	Robert Tannahill (1774–1810), Paisley poet
sneckit	caught		
snell	piercingly; harshly	tap	head
snish tamback	pinch of snuff tobacco	tapsiltoorie	topsy-turvy
		tawpie	foolish
snod	smart, trim	tedder	tether
sonsy	plump, attractive	tent	look after
soy	silk, silken material	tenty	heedful, careful
spae	prophecy, prediction, omen	terr	jaunt, adventure [tear]
spavet	spavined	thicket	thatched
speel'd	climbed	Thomson,	poet (1834–82), b.
speldin	smoked or dried haddock	James B. V.	Port Glasgow
		thowless	dissolute, ineffectual
spier	ask		
spieran	asking for	thraw	wring
splore	spree, excitement	thrawart	twisted, crooked
spunkie	will-o-the-wisp	throu'ther	confused, mixed up
spurtle	stick for stirring	Thyrsis	a shepherd
stank	gutter grating; semi-stagnant pool	tim	empty
		timoniers	helmsmen
stappit	stuffed, replete	tine	decline
staucher	stagger	tint	lost
stchumers	idiots	tittles	whispers
steer	stir	toom	empty
stell	whisky still	Toonheid	Townhead, district north of Glasgow Cross, near top of High Street
stottin	bouncing		
stour	dust		
stowr'd	rushed		
Strathbungo	south-side district	toozlin'	fondling one another
stridl'd	straddled		
stumpan	boasting	tosh	neat, tidy; dear
sumph	dolt	Toshy	Charles Rennie Mackintosh (1868–1928), Glasgow architect
swats	newly brewed weak beer or a substitute made from molasses, water and yeast		
		trig	neat
		Tron kirk	church beside old public weighing machine (tron) at Glasgow Cross
sweirt	lazy		
swithered	hesitated, dithered		
Symon, Scott	Rangers manager, sacked suddenly		
		Trongate	street west of Glasgow Cross
syne	then		
syvers	drains, gutters	tuim	empty

tuims	empties	wauchle	walk laboriously or clumsily
Tully, Charlie	Celtic footballer (1924–71)	weans	children
twarie	two	weary-fa	the devil take . . .
twin	meander, wind about	web-glass	magnifying glass for examining web of cloth
tyne	lose		
tynt	lost	wecht	weight
		Wee Kirk	Tron Church
ugsome	disgusting, horrible	weim	belly, stomach
unco	very; strange	wersh	tasteless, insipid
urny	aren't	West-port	well in Argyle Street, its water famous for making punch
vogie	arrogant, vain		
VP	cheap wine		
		wheecht	whipped
wa	wall	wheen	a good few
wabbit	worn	wicht	person
wabster	weaver	Wilson	Alexander Wilson (1766–1813), Paisley poet and ornithologist
wae	woe		
waerife, waukrife	sleepless		
waeroom	weigh-room		
waesuck	alas	wizzent	wizened
waled	picked, chosen	wulkies, tummle	
wame	stomach	thur	somersault (tumble like wildcats)
wardlin	wordling		
ware	spend	wynds	narrow lanes
warsslan	wrestling, struggling	wyne	command (to horse, etc) to turn left
watergaw	indistinct rainbow		
		yill	ale

Index of Poets

Further Reading

William Donaldson, 'Popular Literature: The Press, the People, and the Vernacular Revival'
in *The History of Scottish Literature*, vol. 3, nineteenth century, ed. Douglas Gifford
(Aberdeen: Aberdeen University Press, 1988), pp.203–15.

Douglas Dunn, 'Silence from Farm and Suburb' (review of *Identities*). *Poetry Review* 71:4,
December 1981, pp.55–56.

George Eyre-Todd, *The Glasgow Poets: their lives and poems* (Glasgow and Edinburgh:
William Hodge, 1903; 2nd ed., Paisley: Alexander Gardner, 1906).

Joseph Fisher, *The Glasgow Encyclopedia* (Edinburgh: Mainstream, 1993).

Robin Hamilton, 'Myself and Poetry' in *Akros* 16:48, December 1981, pp.50–52.

Philip Hobsbaum, 'A City Used by Artists' (review of *Noise and Smoky Breath*) in *Glasgow
Magazine*, 3, Autumn 1983, pp.30–33.

J. A. Hammerton, 'Poetry in Glasgow' in *Sketches from Glasgow* (Glasgow and Edinburgh:
John Menzies, 1893), pp.143–55.

James A. Kirkpatrick, *Literary Landmarks of Glasgow* (Glasgow: Saint Mungo Press, 1898).

Tom Leonard, 'On Reclaiming the Local and the Theory of the Magic Thing' in *Edinburgh
Review*, 77, May 1987, pp.40–46.

Tom Leonard, ed., *Radical Renfrew: Poetry from The French Revolution to The First World
War by poets born, or sometime resident in, the County of Renfrewshire* (Edinburgh:
Polygon, 1990).

Farquhar McLay, ed., *Workers City* (Glasgow: Clydeside Press, 1988).

Farquhar McLay, ed., *The Reckoning* (Glasgow: Clydeside Press, 1990).

Mitchell Library, Glasgow, *Catalogue of the Scottish Poetry Collection*.

Edwin Morgan, 'Glasgow Speech in Recent Scottish Literature' in *Scotland and the Lowland
Tongue*, ed. J. Derrick McClure (Aberdeen: Aberdeen University Press, 1983),
pp.195–208.

Edwin Morgan, 'Glasgow Writing' in *Books in Scotland* 15, Summer 1984, pp.4–6.

Edwin Morgan, *Glasgow Poets Past and Present: The Story of a City* (Hamilton, NZ:
University of Waikato Department of English, 1993) (Avizandum Editions No.1).

Stephen Mulrine, 'Poetry in Glasgow Dialect' in *Focus on: Scotland*, ed. Manfred Görlach
(Amsterdam/Philadelphia: John Benjamins Publishing, 1985), pp.226–35.

Hugh Quigley, ed., *Lanarkshire in Prose and Verse* (London: Elkin Mathews & Marrot, 1929).

Geddes Thomson, ed., *Identities: an anthology of West of Scotland poetry, prose and drama*
(London: Heinemann, 1981).

Hamish Whyte, 'Local Poetry' in *Scottish Culture: The Local Dimension*, ed. Don Martin
(Motherwell: Scottish Library Association, 1991), pp.36–48.